THE NON-PROPHET'S GUIDE™ TO THE RAPTURE

Written & Illustrated by

TODD HAMPSON

HARVEST PROPHECY
An Imprint of Harvest House Publishers

All emphasis in Scripture quotations is added by the author.

Published in association with William K. Jensen Literary Agency, 119 Bampton Court, Eugene, Oregon 97404.

Cover design by Kyler Dougherty

Cover illustration © Todd Hampson

Interior design by Chad Dougherty

For bulk, special sales, or ministry purchases, please call 1-800-547-8979.
Email: CustomerService@hhpbooks.com

The Non-Prophet's Guide™ to the Rapture

Published by Harvest House Publishers
Eugene, Oregon 97408
www.harvesthousepublishers.com

ISBN 978-0-7369-8389-1 (pbk)
ISBN 978-0-7369-8390-7 (eBook)

Library of Congress Control Number: 2025937065

Printed in Colombia

25 26 27 28 29 30 31 32 33 34 / NI / 10 9 8 7 6 5 4 3 2 1

To Luke Hampson, my youngest son. Your quiet strength, resilience during adversity, compassionate care for others, along with your zest for adventure, will be great tools in the hands of the Lord. I could not be more proud of you, and I am so thankful to be your dad. Keep pursuing the Lord and rest in his perfect provision.

Acknowledgments

Thank you to my wife, Tracey, for your constant support and encouragement throughout this entire book series and beyond. I have been blessed beyond measure with you by my side, and I am forever thankful for the life that we have built together, the children we raised, and the amazing adventures yet in our future—until the Lord returns or calls us home.

CONTENTS

SECTION 4: The Bottom Line

SECTION 5: The Best News Ever

INTRODUCTION

And Still...

We wait for the blessed hope—the appearing of the glory of our great God and Savior, Jesus Christ.

TITUS 2:13

This was the moment he had been preparing for since the age of seven. All the years of training—the blood, the sweat, and the tears—for this moment. There was nothing more left to do. The contest was over, and now, the results were in someone else's hands. The sound of his own heavy breathing, combined with the whoosh-whoosh of his heart beating in his ears, muffled the satisfied cheers and chatter of the sold-out crowd.

As his adrenaline dissipated, the exhausted pugilist began to realize how spent his legs felt, how swollen his eyebrow was, and how sore a couple of his ribs were. He looked up into the bright lights to take a deep breath and to receive a squirt of water from the clear plastic bottle his corner team waved in front of him. Then he tilted his head down to catch a glimpse of the blood-stained canvas. He swallowed, and then, exhaled.

After 12 three-minute rounds—a full 36 minutes of laying it all on the line—his heart rate finally began to settle as he watched the referee gather scorecards from the three judges and place them in the hand of the sharply dressed boxing announcer, clad in a tuxedo. The crowd waited in rapt anticipation, quieting to hushed tones in order to hear which fighter would be crowned champion.

At the end of any championship boxing match, there is a pregnant pause—a moment of anticipation as the judges' scorecards are tallied and the announcer awaits the results. When the announcer meticulously reads the three scorecards one at a time, no one yet knows which fighter is the winner. If the contender beat the reigning champion, after reading the scores, the announcer utters these three words, "And the new..." conveying that the former champion has, indeed, lost his belt.

But if the champion wins and retains his belt, after reading the scorecards, the announcer will utter these two words, "And still..." indicating that the champ is still the champ.

When it comes to the primary, epic, and imminent event that church-age believers have been waiting for since the first century, the rapture is still the reigning champion and the pound-for-pound best hope we have. In fact, not only is it the best hope, but it is the blessed hope—*the* event we've all been waiting for and the next event in God's prophetic plan.

The rapture should be on the hearts and minds of every believer, yet it has fallen out of style. Its clear details marred and faded by many persuasive dissenting voices coming from outside of the church and from within. Today, the pretribulational (pretrib) rapture of the church is often seen as a distant cousin to more important doctrines—a once-hyped fantasy of sorts that has lost its luster. Worse yet, the rapture in general, and the pretribulational rapture specifically, is under direct attack from some prominent voices within the church!

So what are Christians to believe? Are those who teach a pretrib rapture abusing Scripture and misleading millions? Is the event merely an invention of a theologian from the 1800s that was popularized in the twentieth century, as many contenders claim? Should Christians retreat to a nebulous, unclear position of panmillennialism and avoid teaching on the topic altogether? After all, everything will pan out in the end, right? Is talk of the end times in general, and teaching about the pretrib rapture specifically, all simply a distracting sideshow for sensationalists? Will the rapture of the church and the return of Christ occur at the same time? What did the early church believe about the rapture? Most importantly, what does God's Word have to say about it?

The purpose of this book is to answer those questions (and many more) with crystal-grade clarity and to reaffirm this important biblical doctrine for a new generation of believers who may be confused or disheartened by the broad assault on the seemingly once-settled truth of the great snatching away (*harpazō* in Greek) of believers. My goal is to demonstrate that this event is clearly prophesied to take place at the end of the church age and that all believers should be looking forward to this momentous event, like a bride anticipating her wedding day.

As one prominent theology expert notes,

> The rapture is often referred to as "the blessed hope" (Titus 2:13) because it provides comfort not only to those believers who are concerned about the coming tribulation, but also to those who long to be reunited with their departed loved ones who share faith in Christ. The second coming, which encompasses both the rapture and the glorious appearing, is one of the most significant events mentioned in the entire Bible. There are 321 references in the New Testament alone to this awesome event, making it the second most prominent doctrine presented in Scripture after the doctrine of salvation.[1]

If the doctrine of the Lord's return is second only to the doctrine of salvation, then it is recognizably a matter of prime importance for our faith and practice as Christians. A careful look at God's inspired, inerrant, authoritative, sufficient, and completed Word makes it abundantly clear that there is no basis for eschatological agnosticism, no reason to throw our hands up and embrace panmillennialism, and no impetus to water down our theological approach due to the direct attacks upon the doctrine of the rapture in general, and the pretrib position in particular. This is a primary biblical topic that all believers should hold in high regard and attempt to understand.

Perhaps this is your first time hearing about the rapture and you simply want to know what it is, where it is found in Scripture, and why it is so important. Whether you are a new believer in Christ who wants to learn the basics of the rapture, or a longtime believer who wants to take a deeper look at the details of this doctrine in order to firmup your convictions and sharpen your apologetic—this book is for you. If we are nearing the end of the church age, as it seems, the fog of spiritual warfare and the crafty deception of the enemy will work to erode our sense of clarity when it comes to this critically important teaching of the Bible.

Therefore, it is time to take an in-depth look at the doctrine of the rapture to show that—despite going 12 championship rounds with various contenders—*it is still*...the undefeated champion, the culmination of our salvation, and the primary end-times event that triggers all the others! Join me in this book as we take a systematic approach, allowing Scripture to be our guide as we discover conclusively that the rapture is present in the Bible. It is our blessed hope, designed to comfort us as we walk through a broken and sinful world and as we await all the promised future events—beginning with the great snatching away of the bride to join her long-awaited Groom.

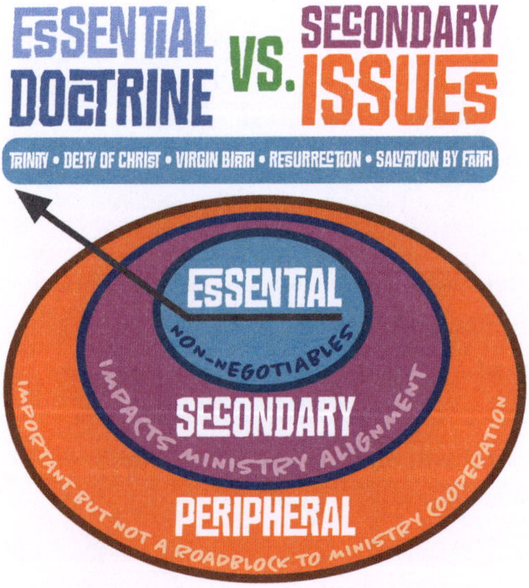

One final note before we dive in. I want to acknowledge the importance of unity in the body of Christ. My goal here is not to intentionally offend my brothers and sisters in Christ who hold to another view of the timing of the rapture (or other end-times events). My goal is to defend what I believe is a critical doctrine for believers to understand and wrestle with—one that I believe is very clear in Scripture when we synthesize all the biblical passages that are related to it. Christians' salvation is based on Christ alone, and while there are fundamental orthodox doctrines that one must hold to in order to be a Christian, your view on the timing of the rapture is not one of them.

That said, I believe the rapture is of extreme importance—perhaps now more than ever. Hebrews 10:25 informs us that watching believers will be able to "see the Day approaching." My friends, the day of the Lord's return at the end of the tribulation is approaching, which means the rapture of the church will come even sooner than that! If the conditions of the world right now, seen through the lens of Scripture and illuminated by the guidance of the Holy Spirit, do not have you convinced that the culmination of the age is near, I am not sure what will. This is why I believe that every believer who is living must come to grips with what Scripture teaches about the rapture.

This is imperative for our generation and for the next generation, whom we are mandated to equip if the Lord does not come in our lifetime. The practical implications of understanding the *timing* of the rapture are immense. It is the difference between preparing for survival during the darkest period of earth's history or preparing for our supernatural wedding day. It is the difference between facing the worst horrors the world has ever seen or seeing the Lord face to face in our glorified bodies, surrounded by millions of other resurrected believers going to the Father's house.

Overall, the purpose of this book is to give believers hope and confidence in the rock-solid doctrine of the rapture, to show the overwhelming support found in Scripture and early church history for the pretribulational rapture position, to demonstrate how the doctrine fits holistically into God's grand narrative, and why this is the most exciting time in history to be alive!

In section 1—The Basics, we will discuss the fundamentals of the rapture as we discover where it is found, how we are to understand it, and when it is going to happen in relation to other end-times events on God's prophetic calendar. We will also consider what Christians have believed during various periods of church history, and we will take a detailed look at ten compelling reasons to believe in a pretribulational rapture.

In section 2—The Backstory, we will take a broader survey of the biblical narrative as we look at all the Old and New Testament accounts of raptures (i.e., people being suddenly removed to heaven or other locations while still alive). We will consider raptures in the Old Testament, raptures in the first century, raptures prophesied for the future, and other key details about what the Bible teaches about the resurrection of the dead and the logical chronology of key end-times events.

In section 3—The Breakdown, we will learn the significance of the Thessalonian church and the importance of Paul's most eschatological letters—1 and 2 Thessalonians. We will take a frame-by-frame, slow-motion look at the details of the rapture from 1 Thessalonians 4, discuss the all-important "removal of the restrainer" from 2 Thessalonians 2, and discover the importance of three key aspects of our salvation and how they relate to the rapture of the church at the end of the church age.

In section 4—The Bottom Line, we will consider the implications for our generation as we witness the convergence of end-times stage-setting conditions in our day, how to get ready for whatever is in our near future, and how to best prepare the next generation of believers to have a solid understanding of eschatology and how to leverage it for the sake of the gospel.

Finally, *in section 5—The Best News Ever*, we will discuss and lay out what it means to be a Christian and why that is the single most important detail every person needs to nail down in their life. Also, we will discuss what all of this means practically for today as we consider how to use our feet before liftoff!

Remember Jesus' promise,

> Do not let your hearts be troubled. You believe in God; believe also in me. My Father's house has many rooms; if that were not so, would I have told you that I am going there to prepare a place for you? And if I go and prepare a place for you, I will come back and take you to be with me that you also may be where I am (John 14:1-3).

And still…!

The Non-Prophet

He's a Renaissance man. The ultimate throwback. The Non-Prophet is a 501(c)(3) that seems to have been born in 501 BC. He prefers the clothing, speech, food, grooming (or lack thereof), and customs of an archetypical Old Testament prophet living in twenty-first-century America. He misunderstands Bible prophecy and gives well-meaning but poor advice. The Non-Prophet is also not very wise with money, so he's a Non-Prophet on two levels. He's the epitome of the idiom "a day late and a dollar short."

SECTION 1:

THE BASICS

GETTING A GRIP ON THE FUNDAMENTALS

CHAPTER 1

Is the Rapture in the Bible?

The Lord himself will come down from heaven, with a loud command, with the voice of the archangel and with the trumpet call of God, and the dead in Christ will rise first. After that, we who are still alive and are left will be caught up together with them in the clouds to meet the Lord in the air. And so we will be with the Lord forever.

1 THESSALONIANS 4:16-17

Every established sport has well-developed fundamentals—foundational skills and techniques that have been developed and refined over time. These fundamentals serve as a key facet of training for beginners and are reinforced continuously thereafter. In football training camps, the pros are reminded of the fundamentals. In boxing, trainers pay attention to the fundamentals and hone the smallest details in order to prepare their fighters and hopefully give them every advantage over their opponent.

So what is the first lesson a boxer learns? Punching? Weaving? Footwork? Nope. The first fundamental skill a boxer needs to master is the boxing stance. The placement and angle of the feet, the weight distribution on the balls of the feet, the appropriate amount of bend in the knees, the specific angle of the waist, the position of the shoulders and elbows, the location and placement of the hands, the angle of the torso, and even the tilt of the head are all key factors that comprise the fundamental boxing stance.

In training, these details are carefully repeated until each one becomes muscle memory. Most fighters must unlearn what their muscles have been taught, and this process takes time and attention. But this training is critical to the success of any serious boxer. To complicate matters, there are various styles of boxing based on a fighter's build, tendencies, and tactics that require modified versions of the basic fundamentals that must be learned.

If a fighter's stance is not developed with strong fundamentals, the rest of his skills will be built on a faulty foundation. The first fundamental a boxer learns may not be the most exciting one, but it is of the utmost importance.

In this section of the book, we are going back to the basics. We're getting our stance correct. If you are new to Bible study, or new to the study of eschatology (the doctrine of things to come), this section is for you. And even if you have studied the topic before, it is good to revisit the fundamentals to make sure your conclusions stand on a solid foundation.

That is why we're beginning this section with a chapter that asks the question, "Is the rapture in the Bible?" Perhaps the title of this chapter took you by surprise. If you are familiar with the doctrine of the rapture and have heard it taught for some time, you may wonder why I propose this question. Well, in addition to revisiting our foundation to make sure we've got it right, believe it or not, there are many today from within the church who attempt to argue that the rapture is not in the Bible. In saying that, sometimes they mean the English word *rapture* is not in the Bible, but there are also those who teach that the very concept of the rapture is not present in the Bible. In this chapter, I will address both of those arguments as we go back to the basics.

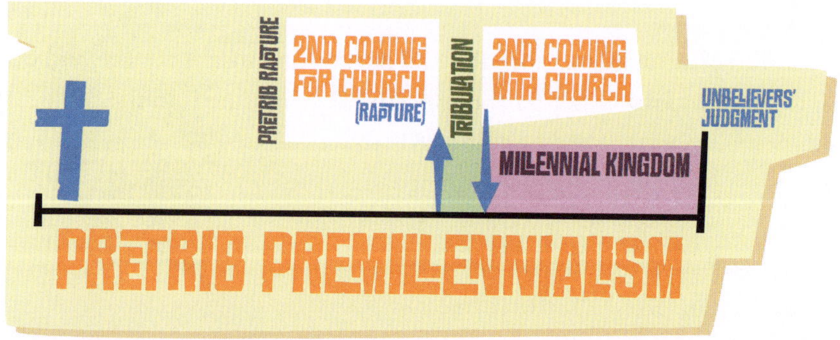

Another related claim is that the doctrine of the pretribulational rapture is a relatively new teaching and that it was made up by a prominent theologian in the 1800s. I'll quite easily bust that myth in chapters 3 and 4. But for now, let's address the question above in both of its forms.

First things first, is the word *rapture* in the Bible? What people are asking here is: Do we find the word *rapture* in the original languages that the Bible was written in? The answer to that question is: No, we do not. Right about here, some would shout, "See! The rapture is not even in the Bible!" But neither is the word *Trinity* or the phrase *Great Commission* for that matter. The word *Bible* is not even in the Bible! So what is going on here?

TOP 3 DEFINITIONS OF HARPAZŌ

1. to seize, carry off by force
2. to seize on, claim for one's self eagerly
3. to snatch out or away

Well, no English words are used in the ancient manuscripts. The real question we need to ask is whether the concept of the rapture is in the Bible. The answer to that is yes! The Greek word *harpazō* is used to describe the moment that we call the rapture. The word simply and clearly (based on all 14 uses in the New Testament) means "to seize," "suddenly take away," or "remove by force." Think of it as a divine snatching away, like a special-ops team extracting a soldier from behind enemy lines.

14XS HARPAZŌ IS USED IN THE NEW TESTAMENT

VERSE	CONNOTATION
Matthew 11:12	taken by violent force
Matthew 12:29	carry off by force
Matthew 13:19	snatching away like a bird snatching a seed
John 6:15	to take by force
John 10:12	like a surprise snatching as from a wolf
John 10:28	to snatch from an open hand without warning
John 10:29	to snatch from an open hand without warning
Acts 8:39	sudden disappearance/vanished from sight
Acts 23:10	urgently grabbed by a soldier and quickly taken away
2 Corinthians 12:2	suddenly caught up to heaven
2 Corinthians 12:4	suddenly caught up to heaven
1 Thessalonians 4:17	suddenly caught up into clouds
Jude 23	quickly rescuing someone from fire
Revelation 12:5	quickly snatched away from immediate danger

Harpazō is the word used in 1 Thessalonians 4:17 (above) that we have translated "caught up" in English Bible translations. The reason it has come to be known as the rapture is because *harpazō* was translated *rapturo* in the Latin translation by Jerome in the late fourth century. Jerome's translation became the standard in the Catholic Church and was used almost exclusively for roughly 1,300 years, until the Reformation in the sixteenth century.

When new English translations were created after the Reformation, the word *rapturo* was simply transliterated as *rapture*. So, no—rapture is not in the Bible, but *harpazō* is. We are not obligated to call it the rapture. We can call it "the great catching away" or "the sudden removal by force" or anything that explains the concept of what is intended by the Greek word *harpazō*. But for simplicity's sake—and because most people understand what is implied by the term—we use the word *rapture*.

The Primary Rapture Texts

In addition to the key passage referenced at the opening of this chapter, where Paul explains the mystery of the rapture in 1 Thessalonians 4, there are a few other New Testament passages that provide additional insight. I'll share two of those in this chapter (1 Corinthians 15:51-53 and John 14:1-3) and one more in chapter 4 (Revelation 3:10), for reasons that will become apparent later.

A *mystery* in the New Testament is not something unknowable. Rather, it is something that was not previously revealed through God's special revelation. This mystery is something that was not shared overtly in the Old Testament. Presumably, Paul learned of this mystery when he himself was caught up to heaven to receive special revelation (more about this in chapter 6).

If you are wondering if an entire doctrine can be developed around a New Testament mystery, the answer is yes. One of the most glaring mystery doctrines is represented by much of the New Testament and nearly 2,000 years of human history. Everything in the New Testament from Acts 2:1 through Revelation 3:22 (as well as Revelation 19:14–22:21) is part of this mystery. This mystery is the church! Believers sometimes forget that the church is a mystery. It is not found in the Old Testament (though there are a few strong hints), yet it was revealed in the New Testament.

We discover other important mysteries in Paul's writings as well. The apostle used the term *mystery* no less than 21 times in his letters. God used at least two supernatural events (Paul's conversion and Paul's trip to heaven) to turn a legalistic persecutor of Christians into the vessel through whom the entire Gentile world would hear the gospel. An incredible amount of Scripture—13 of the 27 New Testament books—came through Paul, the apostle to the Gentiles.

Regarding the mystery of the church, Paul wrote,

> I became a servant of this gospel by the gift of God's grace given me through the working of his power. Although I am less than the least of all the Lord's people, this grace was given me: to preach to the Gentiles the boundless riches of Christ, and to make plain to everyone the administration of this mystery, which for ages past was kept hidden in God, who created all things (Ephesians 3:7-9).

In 2 Corinthians 12:2-4, we find Paul talking about himself in the third person (as an act of humility as supported by the thrust of that chapter); he wrote,

> I know a man in Christ who fourteen years ago was caught up to the third heaven. Whether it was in the body or out of the body I do not know—God knows. And I know that this man—whether in the body or apart from the body I do not know, but God knows—was caught up to paradise and heard inexpressible things, things that no one is permitted to tell.

Regarding the mystery of the rapture, we will first look at 1 Corinthians 15:51-53, where the apostle Paul wrote,

> Listen, I tell you a mystery: We will not all sleep, but we will all be changed—in a flash, in the twinkling of an eye, at the last trumpet. For the trumpet will sound, the dead will be raised imperishable, and we will be changed. For the perishable must clothe itself with the imperishable, and the mortal with immortality.

Here we have Paul revealing for the first time, the doctrine of the rapture. We're not given all the details of this future event, but we are clearly given two specific details that I would like to address in this chapter (later, in chapter 4, I'll address the trumpet detail). First, we are told, "We will not all sleep" (verse 51). While those of you with young children may think this is a prophecy about your children at bedtime, it is actually a common euphemism for death found in the New Testament.

Believers who fall asleep (using the imagery for earthly death) simply close our eyes in this world and open them in heaven. We're told that to be absent from the body is to be present with the Lord (2 Corinthians 5:8). Throughout Paul's epistles, he often refers to death as sleep. So the idea in 1 Corinthians 15 is that we will not all die. The final generation of Christians in the church age will not see death but will be transformed—given their glorified bodies in an instant. By the way, my good friend and Greek scholar Jeff Kinley often shares that the Greek word that we translate "in a moment" is *atomos*, from which we get the English word for atom. It is an indivisible moment of time.

The closest thing to this in our modern vernacular is Planck time. This unit of time is taken from studies in theoretical physics and was discovered by Max Planck in the late 1800s. It was shared in a scientific paper by him in 1899.[1] Planck time is (in modern human terms) the shortest measurable unit of time. For all we know, God's atomos could be even shorter than our modern Planck time, but the point is that this change from our natural bodies to our glorified spiritual bodies will be instantaneous. While this may seem impossible to us, nothing is impossible for the God who created everything out of nothing.

The second detail from 1 Corinthians 15 that I want to point out is this: Those who have died in the church age (those who sleep in Christ) will be resurrected at this time. Notice Paul wrote, "The dead will be raised imperishable, and we will be changed" (verse 52). The context of the chapter is the resurrection of church-age believers. On a side note, please do not miss the fact that Paul assumed the Lord would return during his lifetime. Note the phrase "we will be changed."

The promise of the gospel is for our born-again spirits as well as the redemption of our sin-marred bodies! Our spiritual salvation is the down payment for our full redemption as image bearers. We are created in the image of God as a complex union of body and spirit. Unlike the false teaching of the Gnostics in the New Testament (and the many other times this ancient heresy has reared its ugly head throughout church history), the human body is not evil. It was created by God. All humans (saved or unsaved) are created in the image of God and include a glorious and complex union of body and spirit.

The Promises from Jesus

With the primary rapture passages of 1 Thessalonians 4:13-18 and 1 Corinthians 15:51-53 in mind, let us now take a look at a key moment in the ministry of Jesus. As he neared the events of the cross, he wanted to provide his disciples one final comforting message. In what has come to be known as the upper room discourse—found only in the Gospel of John (chapters 13–14)—we become like flies on the wall during Jesus' final teaching to his disciples before he would be betrayed and crucified. Immediately following the last supper and his teaching in the upper room, Jesus and the disciples went to the garden of Gethsemane—the final stop before Jesus' arrest.

In John 13, we find this final teaching already in progress while Jesus was washing the disciples' feet. Jesus shot straight with the twelve, telling them he would be betrayed by one of them, and that Peter would disown him three times before the night was over. With those jarring proclamations fresh in the minds of his disciples, Jesus then spoke great words of comfort to them. In the opening verse of John 14, Jesus stated, "Do not let your hearts be troubled. You believe in God; believe also in me" (verse 1).

After Jesus' fear-calming statement, he then shared a promise to return and a promise to take the disciples (and us) with him. In verses 2-3, we read this incredibly revealing and hope-filled prophecy: "In My Father's house are many mansions; if it were not so, I would have told you. I go to prepare a place for you. And if I go and prepare a place for you, I will come again and receive you to Myself; that where I am, there you may be also" (NKJV).

At first glance, this may not seem relevant to the topic at hand. The rapture was a mystery until Paul, inspired by the Holy Spirit, wrote down the revelation he had received concerning the event. But if we compare Jesus' statements in this passage with Paul's statements from the key rapture text cited at the beginning of this chapter, we find an amazing correlation between the two. I believe this confirms the two passages are talking about the same event.

1 THESSALONIANS 4:17-18

Then we who are alive, who remain, will be caught up together with them in the clouds **to meet the Lord in the air,** **and so we will always be with the Lord.** Therefore, **comfort one another** with these words. (NASB)

JOHN 14:1-3

Do not let your heart be troubled; believe in God, believe also in Me. In My Father's house are many rooms; if that were not so, I would have told you, because I am going there to prepare a place for you. And if I go and prepare a place for you, **I am coming again and will take you to Myself,** **so that where I am, there you also will be.** (NASB)

We are given two promises in John 14:2-3: (1) Jesus himself left to go and prepare a place for us, and (2) he is going to come again and receive us to himself. Let's take a closer look at these promises:

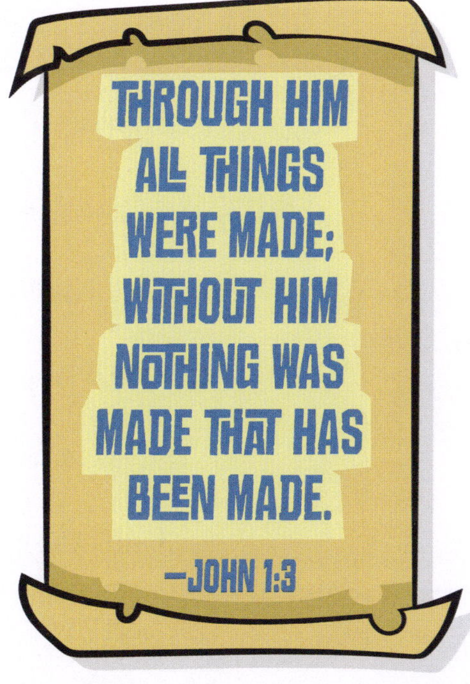

Going to Prepare a Place

First, Scripture tells us that all of creation was made through Jesus. He was also a carpenter by trade before he began his earthly ministry. If it took him six days to create the heavens and the earth, can you imagine how amazing our future place is going to be? What meticulous care and attention to personal detail must be given to something that takes Jesus 2,000 years to build?

Coming Back to Receive Us

Second, Jesus promised that he is coming back to receive us. He's not just coming back to us. He's also receiving us—that is, we're also going to him. In other words, he's meeting us somewhere in the middle. Indeed, the final step in the ancient Jewish wedding tradition was what was known as the *nissuin* ("to take"). The term comes from *naso*, which literally means "to lift up!"[2] In 1 Thessalonians 4, we are given many more details, as well as the exact order of events related to the rapture. We will look at this in great detail in chapter 10.

Some have argued that Jesus is simply describing his return at the judgment—that John 14:1-3 is describing the same event as Revelation 19:11-15. But a simple comparison of the details quickly reveals to us that these are two vastly different events.

Feet Firmly Planted

Circling back to our opening analogy of a boxer learning the basics, beginning first and foremost with a proper stance—we can stand firm in our knowledge that the concept of the rapture is indeed taught in Scripture. Not only is it taught, but if we slow down long enough and look carefully, we find that we are given quite a bit of detail about this promised future event.

Furthermore, we discover that it is not merely an obscure or nebulous teaching. It is, in fact, of such importance that Paul—the apostle to the Gentiles—was given special revelation on the matter. If that were not enough, our Lord Jesus himself shared the foundational promise of the rapture with his disciples as he comforted them with his final teaching before the crucifixion. In fact, both Jesus and Paul cited the natural comfort that the teaching of the great catching away was intended to bring:

> Jesus: "Do not let your hearts be troubled" (John 14:1).
>
> Paul: "Therefore, comfort one another with these words" (1 Thessalonians 4:18 NASB).

CHAPTER 2

When Will the Rapture Happen?

And to wait for his Son from heaven, whom he raised from the dead—Jesus, who rescues us from the coming wrath.

1 THESSALONIANS 1:10

After a boxer has the fundamental aspects of the boxing stance down, they learn basic punches and footwork. These are key for both offense and defense, but there is one underlying element that is critical to their success—timing!

A boxer can display great form in punches and footwork, but without a sense of timing they are predictable, and their offense can be nullified by the opponent. Knowing when to throw a certain punch or combination is vital to landing key shots. Knowing when to use footwork is critical to controlling range, circling away from the opponent's power shots, and stepping in to deliver the right combination at the right time.

In short, timing is absolutely critical. This is true in boxing, and this is true with the rapture. With the clear understanding that the rapture *will* happen, now the question is, when? Specifically, *when* in relationship to the tribulation period. Will it happen prior to the beginning of this future seven-year time of God's active, long-prophesied judgment of the nations? Will the rapture happen part of the way into it, halfway into it, toward the end, or at the very end, when Christ returns? These are the various views that are held.

Again, if prominent theologians hold to differing views on this matter, how can we really know? Well, as you'll see in the next few chapters, not only can we know for certain, but it is imperative that we wrestle with the relevant sections of Scripture until we do know. Imagine for a moment if we are indeed on the cusp of the tribulation period (Daniel 9:27; Matthew 24; Revelation 6–19). Our understanding of end-times events greatly affects our outlook, emotions, decisions, actions, and focus. Practically speaking, there is a monolithic difference in how we live right now, based on our view of the timing of the rapture. Much depends on whether we escape God's active wrath on earth—or whether we must live through some or all of it. There can only be one correct view. Thankfully, God is not silent on the matter.

Before we get to the various views of the timing of the rapture, there is a broader issue to consider first—interpretation methods. To do so, we need to pull the camera back a bit further. We must first establish a fundamental premise—the entire Bible is special revelation that was inspired (lit. *God-breathed*) by God (2 Timothy 3:16). To be more specific, I believe in the verbal plenary inspiration of Scripture. By that I mean I believe *every word* in the Bible is intentional and inspired by God, including *every part* of the Bible.

2 TIMOTHY 3:16

All Scripture is inspired by God and beneficial for teaching, for rebuke, for correction, for training in righteousness.

INSPIRED = [LIT.] GOD-BREATHED
VERBAL = EVERY WORD
PLENARY = FULL/COMPLETE

While there have been recent attempts by influential evangelical leaders to undermine various parts of the Bible—it is an all-or-nothing proposition. Either the entire Bible is inspired, or we have no idea what is truly from God.

In the latter case, individuals become the ultimate authority—deciding what is actually from God and what can be discarded.

There have been many once-orthodox seminaries that have gone off the rails theologically—and in each case their downfall began with a weakening stance on the inerrancy of Scripture. Throughout church history, Satan's two-fold attack on Christians has been through persecution from the outside and false teaching from within. The inside battle always begins with the erosion of the doctrine of inerrancy. The serpent always begins his inner attack by asking the same question he posed to Eve in Genesis 3:1, "Has God really said…?" (NASB).

This ancient lie comes in various forms in our day. There are prominent figures today who say the Genesis account is allegorical, that we can ignore the Old Testament, that the only words that we need to take to heart are those of Jesus in the New Testament, or that the Bible merely contains the Word of God. The Bible does not contain the Word of God—the Bible *is* the Word of God. It is all-or-nothing. With that established, let us turn our attention to the question of interpretation.

Historical Interpretation Methods for Eschatology

Throughout church history, theologians have used one of four interpretation methods. Some of the methods allegorize or spiritualize Scripture—stripping eschatology from its literal meaning (idealism, historicism). While another concludes that the events described in Revelation (all except the return of Christ) already took place in AD 70, when Rome attacked Jerusalem (preterism). This method also necessarily allegorizes Revelation and other prophetic passages. And one method interprets Scripture literally (futurist).

So how should we approach the topic? How can we know which interpretation method to use?

This, my friends, is where we need to apply logic, old-fashioned common sense, and a little bit of sweat equity to study various passages carefully. If you read the four descriptions below and allow Scripture, logic, and the Holy Spirit to guide you, I believe you will see that there is one undeniably clear and correct method that you can use to interpret not only prophecy, but all of Scripture. There is one hermeneutic (Bible study method) that uses the exact same approach from Genesis 1:1 to Revelation 22:21. This simple method allows Scripture to speak plainly and understandably to all people.

Here are the four approaches to eschatology that have been used in church history:

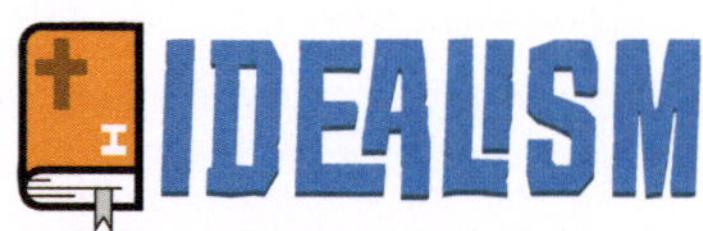

The Idealist View: Prophecy Is Allegory

This school of thought arose around AD 190 from the area of Alexandria, Egypt, and was adopted by the fifth-century theologian Augustine of Hippo. This view became the official church position up to and beyond the Reformation (1517). This view sees Revelation as a general description of the battle between good and evil.

The Preterist View: The Prophecies Already Happened

The preterist view puts forth the notion that the book of Revelation is really just a symbolic picture of first-century events (i.e., the Roman attack on Jerusalem and the destruction of the temple in AD 70), rather than future events that will occur at the end of the church age. Within this framework, there is a spectrum of views ranging from partial to full preterism. But the premise of this view is that what appears to be prophecy in Revelation is actually past history. This method allegorizes Scripture, but it also relies on an early date (AD 64 during Nero's reign) for the writing of the book of Revelation instead of the traditional late date (AD 95 during Domitian's reign) that was held to by the earliest church fathers, including Irenaeus who was the disciple of Polycarp, who was discipled by the apostle John. The idea of an AD 65 date for the writing of Revelation did not appear until AD 508 and is asserted by only two key figures in history as opposed to 15 key figures who assert the late date of the writing of Revelation beginning as early as AD 150.[1]

The Historicist View: Prophecy Is Merely an Overview of History

This view first appeared around AD 300 and attempts to interpret Revelation simply as a symbolic representation of the history of all that has taken place and will take place in church history from John's time to the end. This view was popular during the Reformation era, but has many problems and many versions.

The Futurist View: Prophecy Understood Literally

This view teaches that the end-times prophetic events described in Revelation are yet future and will literally (not symbolically) come to pass. The hundreds of prophecies in the Bible that have already been fulfilled were fulfilled literally, not figuratively. There is no indication anywhere in Scripture that God suggests we switch to a new method of understanding prophecy. A prophecy is given, then at a later time it is fulfilled, just as described. That is the clear nature and pattern of prophecy. The literal interpretation method is inductive, rather than deductive. Inductive study observes the facts and arrives at

conclusions—like a good detective. Deductive study begins with a presupposed idea, then attempts to find support.

When you boil it down, there are really only two categories to choose from when it comes to interpreting end-times Bible prophecy—allegorically or literally.

Either Scripture can be spiritualized—with the interpreter deciding which passages have symbolic meaning—or all of Scripture is meant to be taken literally and understood by the plain and clear meanings of the words themselves (including the clear use of discernable poetic language).

The idealist, preterist, and historicist views all spiritualize (i.e., allegorize) Scripture in some fashion—opening the passage in question to interpretations that may stray from what the original writer intended.

The futurist view is the only approach that maintains a consistent literal understanding of Scripture from beginning to end. Just as fulfilled prophecy was fulfilled literally (including very specific details in many cases), so too will yet-unfulfilled prophecies come to pass exactly as predicted by the plain language of Scripture. More than one prophecy expert has said, "If the plain sense makes sense, seek no other sense, lest you end up with nonsense."

God is not the author of confusion (1 Corinthians 14:33) and he has spoken clearly to us in the Scriptures (2 Timothy 3:16). The Bible was inspired by God to communicate clearly to everyday people. Though some topics in Scripture (such as Bible prophecy and eschatology) take some careful and intentional study, logic and a simple literal understanding is all the approach one needs. No PhDs or church history mastery necessary. The Bible is a supernatural book written for all Christians over all times in all locations—meant to be understood by the laity.

The Views Concerning the Timing of the Rapture

Now, with that necessary point covered, let us shift to the question regarding various views of the timing of the rapture. If we use the literal, futurist interpretation method (described above), then we can easily conclude there is a final seven-year period (Daniel 9:27; Matthew 24:4-31; Revelation 6–19) of God's active judgment on the world.

Daniel 9 is *the* baseline passage where we discover the duration and nature of the tribulation period. All other discussions of the tribulation period (also referred to as the Day of the Lord and the Time of Jacob's Trouble) must begin here and fit within its framework. I cover this in great detail in my book *The Non-Prophet's Guide™ to the Book of Daniel*, but I'll briefly cover the critical intel here. First, it is a time period that specifically focuses on the Jewish people. In Daniel 9:24, we are informed that the span of time prophesied (including the final seven years) are for Daniel's people—the Jewish people.

There are 21 specific judgments prophesied for that period of time. The first five alone—in the opening throes of the tribulation—will result in a quarter of the world's population being killed by war, murder, famine, and disease.

At the time of my writing, the world population is 8,063,911,398[2] (or even higher by other estimates[3]). That means within perhaps only one to two years (there are 14 judgments in the first three and a half years of the future tribulation period), more than 2 billion people will be killed by those early plagues. The current US population is nearing 337 million. Assuming death rates would be similar around the globe, that means more than 84 million people in America would die in the initial judgments of the tribulation period.

Below are the four most commonly held views of the timing of the rapture. While not essential beliefs for salvation, there can logically be only one correct view. Believers should study each view to see what aligns best with the details of Scripture as a whole. Brotherly love along with a spirit of unity and humility should be evident when encountering others who hold to a different view. We are called to be patient and gentle as we teach any area of theology (2 Timothy 2:24).

The Pretribulation View

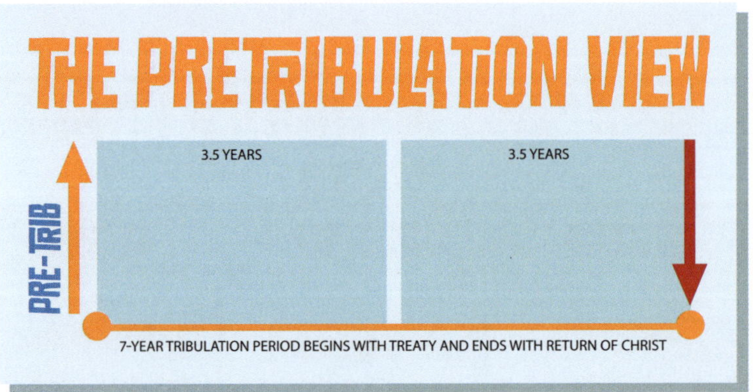

This view holds that the rapture will occur prior to the start of Daniel's seventieth week (1 Thessalonians 5:9-10; Revelation 3:10), that the tribulation period begins with a seven-year peace treaty brokered by the antichrist (Daniel 9:27; 2 Thessalonians 2:3-7), and that Christ will return with the armies of heaven (Zechariah 14:5; Matthew 25:31; 1 Thessalonians 3:13; 2 Thessalonians 1:7; Jude 14; Revelation 19:14) at the end of the seven-year period.

The Mid-Tribulation View

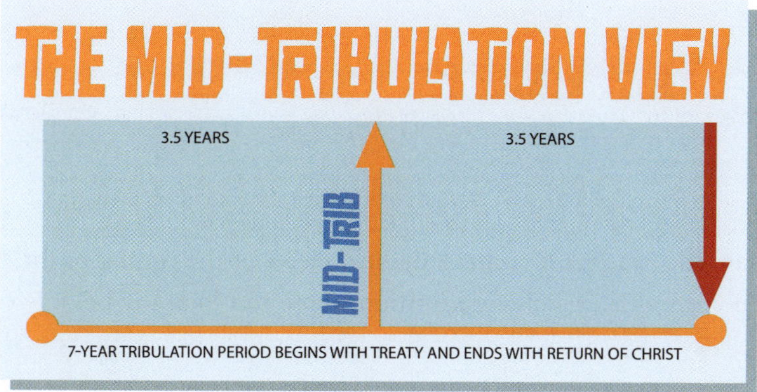

This view holds that Jesus will return at the halfway point of the seven-year tribulation. This halftime point represents the separation between the tribulation and the great tribulation. Here, Jesus' return coincides with the antichrist's invasion of the Jewish temple and the enforcement of the "mark of the beast" (Revelation 12–13).

The Pre-Wrath View

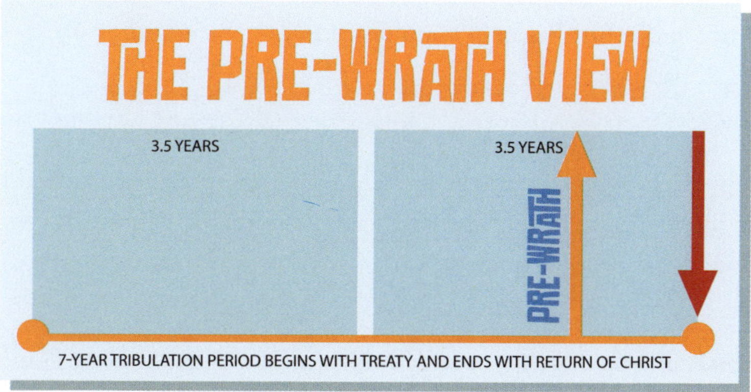

This view holds that the seven seal judgments span the entire seven-year tribulation period (with the other 14 judgments fitting into various places during that time). Also, it asserts that God's wrath does not occur until the sixth seal—roughly five-and-a-half years into the tribulation. Believers are rescued, this view claims, when the sixth seal is opened (Revelation 6:12) and God's wrath begins to be poured out.

The Posttribulation View

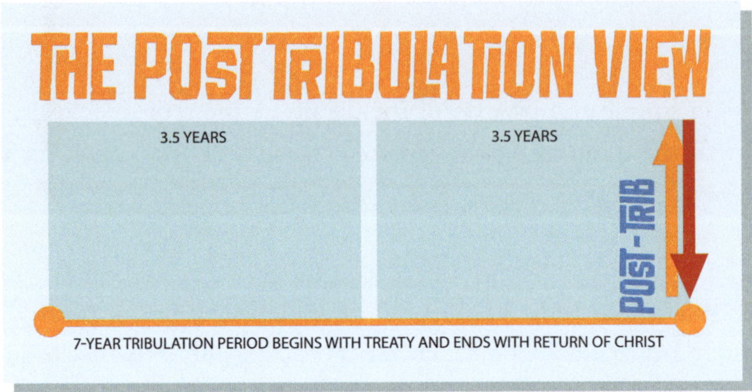

This view holds that Christians will endure all the tribulation and its horrific judgments. They will suffer and be persecuted (and some supernaturally protected) through all this, after which they will be raptured right before Christ returns at his second coming. A variation of this view surmises that the events of the tribulation are merely allegorical of the trials of the church age and that the rapture and return happen simultaneously at the end of history.

The Views Concerning the Millennial Kingdom

Below are the four most commonly held views about the nature and timing of the millennial kingdom. I used to cover only the first three, but in recent years a fourth has become quite prominent and is worth taking time to address:

Amillennialism

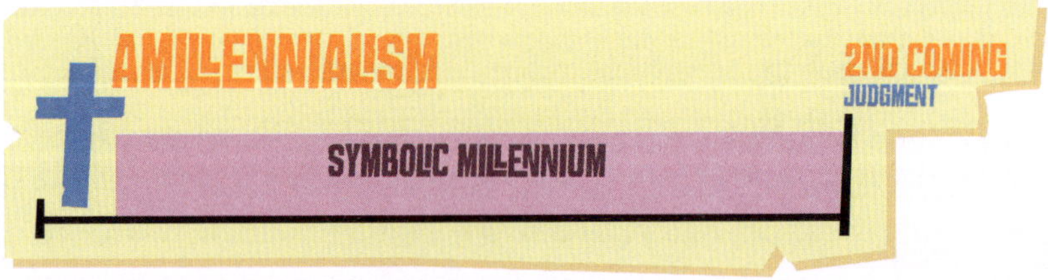

This view holds that the millennium is not a literal 1,000-year period but is merely symbolic of the entire church age, with Christ returning at some time in the future. This is the most widely held view across denominations. Also, many who hold to this view believe that the rapture passages (1 Corinthians 15:52 and 1 Thessalonians 4:13-17) are merely describing the resurrection at the return of Christ. They typically view the rapture/resurrection as a simultaneous event with the return of Christ.

However, a simple comparison of the details of the rapture and the return dictate that these must be two separate events (yet both part of the return). As one theologian puts it,

> This "coming" (Gr. parousia, lit. appearing) of Christ is the same as His appearing in the clouds (cf. Acts 1:11). It is not His Second Coming, which will occur at the end of the Tribulation. That is a separate coming at which time He will remain on the earth, set up His earthly kingdom, and reign for 1,000 years (cf. Rev. 19:11-21). The differences in the descriptions of these comings present them as separate events (cf. Matt. 24:30-31 and 1 Thess. 4:15-17).[4]

The first advent had two key aspects. We celebrate them each year as Christmas and Easter. Similarly, the second advent will involve two key aspects—the rapture to meet Jesus in the atmosphere and the physical return of Jesus to earth.

Postmillennialism

This view holds that the church will so evangelize the world that it will usher in the second coming of Christ. This view became increasingly popular during the great missionary movements of the eighteenth and nineteenth centuries, but largely fell out of favor after World War I and World War II, when people concluded that the world was not actually getting better.

Premillennialism

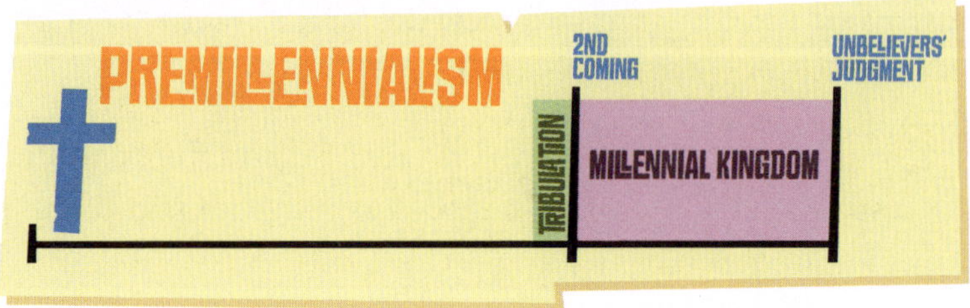

This view holds that Christ will return prior to a literal, future 1,000-year kingdom ruled by the Savior. This view sees God's unconditional promises to Abraham and David as literal with their ultimate fulfillment in a future kingdom where Christ will reign from David's throne and in which Israel will enjoy the full land boundaries originally pledged by God (Genesis 12:1; 15:18-21; 2 Samuel 7:12-16; 1 Kings 4:21).

Panmillennialism

This term first began to show up in evangelical circles around the early 2000s and was originally an attempt to somewhat humorously downplay the differences between end-times views in an attempt to foster unity among believers and avoid controversy. It is similar to what some call the minimalist view. The idea with this view is that we can't really know much about the nature of the end times other than Jesus is coming back and it will all pan out in the end.

However, this view has been adopted by a generation of church leaders who generally see eschatology as a peripheral issue. Many of them not only want to avoid controversy but have personally never studied the topic in enough depth to come to their own conclusions. So while it is true that all true Christians (regardless of their views on the end times) will indeed be with the Lord in eternity, any serious church leader or student of Scripture should reject this view and determine to study eschatology until they adequately teach it to those under their leadership and influence. We are encouraged by the apostle Paul's example to teach the whole counsel of God (Acts 20:27). Though Paul was with the Thessalonian believers for only around three weeks, he taught them all of the key details of eschatology.

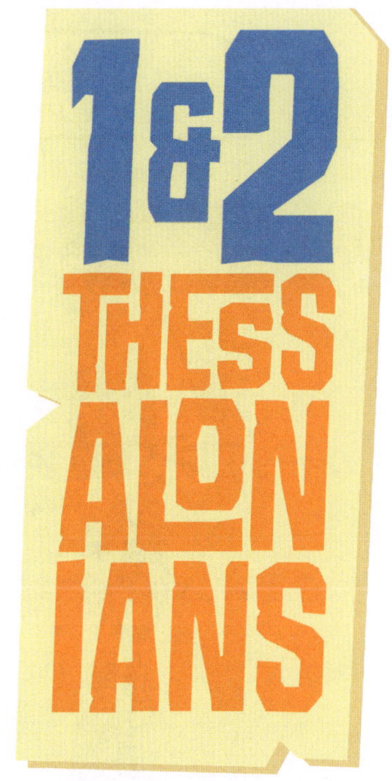

Will the Real View, Please, Stand Up?

I believe an inductive study of Scripture with the premise that all of God's Word is inspired and authoritative very clearly leads to a pretribulational view of the rapture and a premillennial view of the return of Christ. The church age will officially end when the bride is whisked away via the rapture, and the Lord will return at the end of a literal seven-year period to usher in a literal 1,000-year kingdom on earth as an overture to eternity.

I know people who love the Lord as much as I do who hold to other views, and I do not suppose that I have every single detail of our prophesied future completely correct. But I am thoroughly convinced that the pretribulational, premillennial view is the single correct view—and that the literal futurist interpretation method is the single correct approach to understanding Scripture from cover to cover.

Now you may be thinking, *What are the strengths of the pretribulation rapture position?* I will address that question in chapter 4, but first, let us take a quick trip through church history to see what people have believed over the years about the timing of the rapture and what influenced their perspectives.

Church History and the Rapture

You do not lack any spiritual gift as you eagerly wait for our Lord Jesus Christ to be revealed.

1 CORINTHIANS 1:7

While many people (understandably) view boxing simply as an event where two people violently punch each other, those who have studied the sport or trained as a boxer refer to it as the sweet science. This term was coined by British sportswriter Pierce Egan in 1813.[1] His point was that boxing requires a scientific approach—a careful study of the opponent. All other things being equal, the bout is more of a chess match than a violent display of punches. The winner of an equally matched bout (which is the goal of legitimate matchups) must possess the higher ring IQ than their opponent in order to come out on top.

But this sweet science took time to develop. The boxing that exists today—which is much safer than in times past—has its roots in the ancient world and has progressed over time as it has become more formalized and regulated.

Between ancient and modern times, certain milestones helped facilitate the progression of boxing. A brief overview of the history of boxing helps demonstrate this process of systemization. Archeological discoveries reveal that pugilism (from the Latin word *pugil*, equivalent to our English word *boxer*) has been around as far back as 5,000 years ago as evidenced by Sumerian relief carvings. Archeologists have also uncovered Egyptian and Middle Eastern depictions of boxing that date from between 1500–1350 BC. Various records from Greek history show that formalized boxing was part of their culture. In fact, the fighting sport became a formal Olympic event in 688 BC as part of the twenty-third Olympiad. As one would expect, these contests took on a much more brutal tone during the days of the Roman Empire. The contests were organized as sporting events as well as fight-to-the-death gladiator spectacles.[2]

The apostle Paul was familiar with the sport in ancient times. His hometown of Tarsus had a thoroughly Greek culture, and the apostle would have been very familiar with the Isthmian Games, which were the precursor to the Olympic Games. We notice in Scripture that Paul used boxing and foot-racing analogies in some of his letters.

In 1 Corinthians 9:25-27, he wrote,

> Everyone who competes in the games goes into strict training. They do it to get a crown that will not last, but we do it to get a crown that will last forever. Therefore I do not run like someone running aimlessly; I do not fight like a boxer beating the air. No, I strike a blow to my body and make it my slave so that after I have preached to others, I myself will not be disqualified for the prize.

Though pugilism has been around since the earliest of historical records, modern boxing as we know it grew out of English bare-knuckle fighting. Eventually, gloves and other protections were added as the sport became more formalized. Overall, the sport was broadly influenced by what are known as the Marquess of Queensberry rules, first published in 1867 (and built upon the earlier London Prize Ring rules from 1838). The Queensberry rules were written by British Amateur Athletic Club member John Graham Chambers, and they were endorsed by John Sholto Douglas, the Ninth Marquess of Queensberry—hence the name.[3]

There are 12 basic rules, and most of them are logical and commonly held to, though a few are quite comical. For example, rule number 5 states, "A man

hanging on the ropes in a helpless state, with his toes off the ground shall be considered down." Another one, rule number 11, states there shall be "no shoes or boots with springs allowed."[4]

Both the London Prize Ring rules and the later Marquess of Queensberry rules facilitated the rapid spread of boxing in both Great Britain (which was near the height of the British Empire at the time) and the United States—making it a global sport with rules for both amateur and professional boxers.

As the sport developed, international tournaments began. These were often annual events, biennial events, or—as with the Olympics—held every four years. The most well-known of these international events are the European Games, the Commonwealth Games, the Pan American Games, the African Games, and the World Military Games. These international events are governed by an entity formed in 1946 known as the Association Internationale de Boxe Amateur (AIBA).[5] Today, it is known as the International Boxing Association (IBA).

As boxing developed, it became a lucrative sport for the few who made it to the top. This became a draw for anyone of little means to put it all on the line for the chance to win big. In the modern boxing era, four sanctioning bodies for professional boxing were formed in the 1960s, 1970s, and 1980s. The World Boxing Association (WBA) in 1962, The World Boxing Council (WBC) in 1963, and the International Boxing Federation (IBF) in 1977. Later, in 1988, The World Boxing Organization (WBO) was formed, but it was not fully recognized until 2004.[6]

Now you may be asking yourself, *What in the world does the history of boxing have to do with the history of the doctrine of the rapture?* As you will see, the doctrine of the rapture had a raw and basic ancient form that was developed over time. The formalization of theology did not come neatly packaged in a divinely revealed set of canonical endnotes. It was forged through church history as various heresies arose.

The famous creeds that serve as milestones in church history were developed as influential theologians of the day came together to address heretical teaching that threatened to undermine Scripture and the gospel. For example, the Nicene Creed of AD 325 is a time-tested creed that was formulated in response to the heresy of Arianism, which challenged that Jesus was a created being and therefore not divine in nature. The creed has stood the test of time, culture, and theological swings to help keep a level of orthodoxy (what Christians should believe) and orthopraxy (how Christians should behave) in Christendom. As a summary of core fundamental beliefs of the Christian faith, the Nicene-Constantinopolitan Creed of AD 381 has helped maintain commonality and theological understanding among believers all over the world, keeping the church tethered to the core fundamental teachings of the Bible.

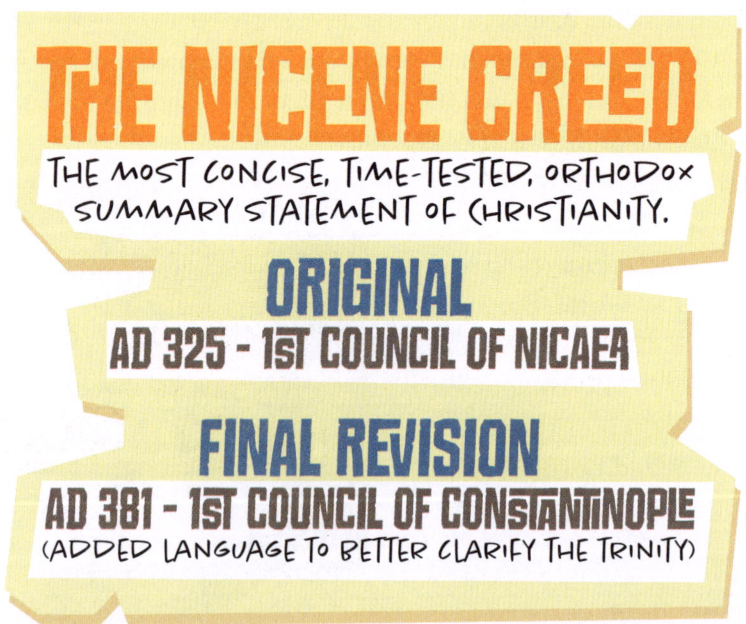

The Protestant Reformation came about in response to abuses in the church and the false teaching promoting salvation by faith plus works. Out of this came the clarification of soteriology, or the doctrine of salvation. In many ways, church history is the messy record of core Christian doctrines being defended and clarified from Scripture.

Join me on a brief drive through church history to see the development of eschatology. As you will see from the survey of history below, first-century believers held a raw, undeveloped pretribulational view of the rapture. While an understanding of church history is not needed to interpret the Bible, it does shed light on why theologians approached eschatology differently during various periods of church history.

History of Eschatology

Ancient Pretribulationism

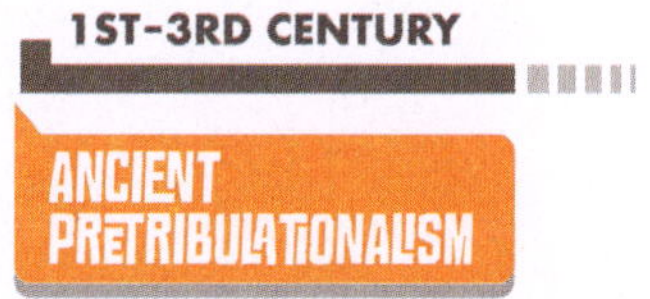

The early church was focused on spreading the gospel and trying to survive the intense persecution faced during the first four centuries AD. Though not formalized in a systematic fashion, the concept of a pretribulation rapture existed and was broadly accepted in the earliest church period following the deaths of the apostles.

For example, early church records demonstrate that Polycarp (AD 69–155) was a direct disciple of John the Apostle (AD 6–100), who wrote five books in the New Testament, including the book of Revelation around AD 95. Irenaeus (circa AD 130–201) was a direct disciple of Polycarp. Irenaeus held and taught a pretribulational rapture.[7]

In AD 180, Irenaeus crafted his great work *Against Heresies* to combat the heretical teachings of Gnosticism, which greatly threatened orthodox doctrine at the time. He wrote,

> And therefore, when in the end the Church shall be suddenly caught up from this, it is said, "There shall be Tribulation such as has not been since the beginning, neither shall be."[8]

Notice the progression and chronology. Irenaeus taught that the church would be suddenly caught up, then the tribulation period would commence.

The Didache (also known as *The Teaching of the Twelve*), the earliest known doctrinal statement document (circa AD 70–100) outside of the Bible, also displays a clear pretribulational stance using a few primary arguments. One of them being that the Lord could return at any time and we must always be ready (what we would call the doctrine of imminency). Another being that Christians will return with Christ at the second coming and that there are two separate resurrections for believers (what we would call the church prior to the tribulation period, then, the Old Testament and tribulation saints at the end of the tribulation period).[9] In addition, scholars are discovering many other statements made by the early church that demonstrate they held to an unformalized, but clear, pretribulational view.

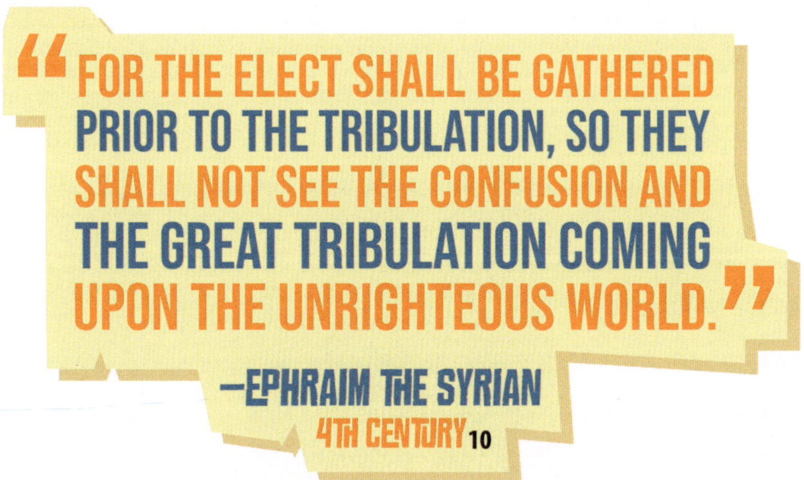

It is also important to note here that the early church was premillennial. As one author notes, "Papias, Justin Martyr, Irenaeus, Victorinus, and other early church fathers held a literal view of the thousand years (called 'chialism' in their time, from the Greek word for 'thousand'). This view prevailed for the first three hundred years of the Church."[11]

Another scholar highlights this fact as well. Referring to the early church period (AD 100–500) as the Patristic Period, Michael Svigel writes, "In the period immediately following the age of the apostles (AD 30–100), the early church continued to anticipate the soon return of Jesus Christ...Along with this expectation of the soon return of Christ as judge and king, many early Christians understood the prediction of the thousand-year reign of Christ on earth in Revelation 20 as a future earthly period that would follow Christ's return and the resurrection of the righteous (premillennialism)."[12]

I find it very compelling that those closest to the time of the apostles held a form of pretribulationalism and were thoroughly premillennial—believing in a literal 1,000-year reign of Christ.

Eschatology in the Middle Ages—Idealism

A spiritualized view of Scripture arose around AD 190, originating from Alexandria, Egypt. This view was adopted by the fourth-century theologian Augustine of Hippo. Augustine applied this spiritualization only to prophetic texts, unlike the Alexandrians, who applied it to all of Scripture.

We can sympathize with Augustine's willingness to switch to an allegorical interpretation method when it came to yet-unfulfilled prophecy, because much of it centers around Israel and the Jewish people. In Augustine's lifetime, Israel had not been a nation for nearly three centuries and the Jewish people had been expelled from the land. We can also respect the fact that Augustine pushed back on the allegorical interpretation method for all other areas of theology.

Augustine's teaching became the dominant view of the early Roman Catholic Church and remained so until the sixteenth century. Dissenting views were considered heretical. Many people were killed for teaching doctrine that did not line up with the official Roman Catholic views. Any writings that taught other views (if found) were likewise destroyed. This interpretation method leads to amillennialism (there is no literal future kingdom), replacement theology (that the church has replaced Israel), and a figurative view of the tribulation period, but a literal return of Christ.

Eschatology of the Reformation—Historicism

1ST CENTURY — ANCIENT PRETRIBULATIONALISM
4TH CENTURY — ESCHATOLOGY IN THE MIDDLE AGES: IDEALISM
1517 — ESCHATOLOGY OF THE REFORMATION: HISTORICISM...AND...

Key figures of the Protestant Reformation, such as Martin Luther and John Calvin, did a great service to Christians everywhere by reforming many of the teachings of the established church—primarily the doctrine of salvation through Christ alone (*solus Christus*), by grace alone (*sola gratia*), through faith alone (*sola fide*), but also the other key *solas* (Scripture alone [*sola scriptura*] and to God's glory alone [*soli Deo gloria*]). Unfortunately, the reformers did not apply this return to a literal interpretation to the events surrounding the return of Christ.

The only New Testament book for which Calvin

did not write a commentary was the book of Revelation, and Luther did not use the final book of the Bible in his preaching and teaching. The reformers viewed the book as a symbolic overview of church history, and they connected the Roman Catholic Church with any negative symbolism of the book. So initially the reformers used the allegorical historicist approach, but later adopted preterism—oddly enough, from the Catholic tradition (see below).

Eschatology of the Reformation—Preterism

In response to the eschatology of the reformers who connected the negative aspects of eschatology with Catholicism, Catholic theologians developed what is known as the preterist view in an attempt to sway popular belief away from post-Reformation teaching. Preterism teaches that the events described in the book of Revelation had already occurred in the first century, when Rome destroyed Jerusalem in AD 70. This is still the primary view of Roman Catholics, and it has also been carried over into some Protestant denominations and Reformed teaching as well.

Preterism teaches that John wrote Revelation prior to AD 70 and that most of the prophecies in Revelation were fulfilled when Rome attacked Jerusalem then. There are many problems with this view, including the necessary allegorizing of Revelation and the fact that the strongest evidence for the timing of the writing of Revelation points to a date of AD 95.

Regarding the writing-date problem with preterism, one prominent expert on the matter notes,

> As even partial preterist Kenneth Gentry admits, there is "strong external witness" that John wrote after AD 70 during Domitian's reign (260). Indeed the earliest witness (Irenaeus) knew Polycarp

(1st cent), the disciple of the apostle John. With him there is an unbroken series of early Fathers who held that John wrote after AD 70 including Irenaeus (2nd cent), Victorinus (3rd cent), and Eusebius (4th cent). The significance of this cannot be overstated. For the early view of John does not destroy the futurist view (that the Tribulation is after AD 70). However, the late view totally destroys the preterist since it is referring to the Tribulation as yet future after AD 70.[13]

There are many other problems with a proposed earlier date for Revelation, particularly related to the letters to the churches in Revelation 2 and 3. For example, the early date for Revelation proposed by preterism means that John would have been a contemporary of Paul, but we know from early church documents that the church of Smyrna (Revelation 2) did not even exist during the ministry of Paul.[14]

Modern Pretribulationalism Premillennialism

Following the Reformation, as more and more people had access to the Bible in their own language, a literal understanding of prophecy returned, leading scholars to conclude that the church could look forward to literal end-times events—including a rebirth of the nation of Israel.

Another key development was the historical period known as the Age of Enlightenment. Many colleges and universities were born out of this period, as were seminaries, and the need arose to further systematize all areas of theology.

In 1830, John Nelson Darby systematized the literal interpretation method along with the pretribulation view of the rapture. In the 1900s, a handful of American theologians (including C.I. Scofield, author of the 1909 Scofield Reference Bible) further popularized the pretribulation view. Then, a few key seminaries holding to the same view were established. These developments eventually made the pretribulational view the dominant view in America among evangelical Christians.

With the reestablishment of Israel as a nation in fulfillment of prophecy, the literal futurist approach has been thoroughly validated. This, and other current conditions that align with a literal understanding of Bible prophecy, has taken pretribulationalism premillennialism to its clearest and most developed form.

Back to the Source

History catalogues development over time. This is true with boxing as well as with theology. Theology is the art and science of determining what God wants to communicate to us through his Word. God's Word never changes, but history and circumstances do. So we can understand why certain doctrines were developed at different points in church history and we can see why various interpretations have arisen at different times.

Although boxing has been formalized and better defined, it remains the same basic sport as it was in its most ancient form—two opponents facing each other for hand-to-hand combat. The same is true with the pretrib rapture. First-century Christians believed the Lord could return at any moment. Early church fathers from the first to the fourth centuries believed in the pretrib rapture.

Most importantly, the Bible clearly teaches a pretrib rapture. Ultimately, it does not matter what gained popularity or how early a particular doctrine was formalized. If that were the case, then salvation through Christ by grace alone, through faith alone (the key tenant of the Reformation) would be suspect because it was not formalized until after 1517! What matters most is determining what God's revealed, inerrant, authoritative, sufficient, and complete Word teaches. It's not the recency of a formal doctrine, but the words of Scripture that determine whether a doctrine is correct. And that is what we will address in chapter 4.

The Strength of the Pretribulation View

Since you have kept my command to endure patiently, I will also keep you from the hour of trial that is going to come on the whole world to test the inhabitants of the earth.

REVELATION 3:10

There is a saying in boxing that "styles make fights." Those three simple words convey a basic reality that each fighter brings something different to the ring and the combination of styles between fighters is what makes a good boxing match exciting. Some boxers are sluggers, some are methodical tacticians, some are flashy showboaters, some are defensive counterpunchers, and some are aggressive pressure fighters. There is a large variety in styles, experience, and approach based on each fighter's unique makeup. Combine any two of the styles above or two of the same style in a boxing match, and you create the potential for an entertaining bout.

But with all the styles, all the variables, all the history, and all the fundamentals, there is one key component that is most critical for every boxer to develop, and what it is may come as a surprise. Most would guess this component would be training regimen, punching technique, defensive guard, counterpunching, strong shoulders, a strong chin, good head movement, or a fit core to absorb body blows. While all of those are essential to boxing, none is as important as one key factor regardless of style, experience, or skill level—the legs!

If a fighter does not have strong, conditioned, well-trained legs—prepared through extensive footwork exercises, muscle memory, and countless miles of running—there is no way they can become a boxing contender, let alone champion. Leg strength and conditioning is a critical component of a boxer's fitness, performance, and ability to go the distance.

A boxer's offense and defense depend on strong legs that can deliver power and conditioning that can weather 12 rounds of footwork used to close distance, change angles, create distance, circle away from an opponent's power range, feint movements, backpedal, and explode forward. Not to mention the essential nature of stable legs when absorbing a hard shot that can buckle knees or drop a boxer to the canvas.

Believe it or not, legs are essential to punching as well. Punches begin their power chain in the toes, work their way up through the legs and the torso, move through the shoulder and elbow, and find their mark with the twist of the wrist and the tightening of the fingers. The best power punches use the entire body from the toes to the fingers.

The energy of a proper punch comes from the ground up, not only from the shoulder. If you watch closely, you'll notice that even the simple jab of a trained boxer begins by pushing off the back foot. For combinations, boxers shift their weight onto one leg or the other, then throw a punch from that side, pushing off from the weighted leg, then they will shift weight to the other leg to throw a punch from that other side.

Well, when it comes to the doctrine of the pretribulational rapture—it has legs! It stands on the solid ground of the clear teaching of Scripture, maintains weight-distributed power in what it teaches, and weathers all the attacks from opponents attempting to knock it down.

While not an essential doctrine for salvation, the pretrib rapture doctrine is nonetheless an extremely important core tenet of the Christian faith and our salvation. The rapture of the church will be the conclusion of the sealing of the Holy Spirit after each believer receives Christ; the promised return of the Bridegroom to take his bride to the Father's house; the rescue of the beloved before the wrath of God falls; and the imminent event that believers have longed for since the first century. It is our blessed hope!

I want to share the top ten reasons to believe in the pretrib rapture below, but first, I want to take the opportunity to address two of the most common arguments I hear when people come against the pretrib doctrine.

Two Common Arguments Against the Doctrine of the Pretrib Rapture

Common Argument #1

One of the most common arguments against the pretrib rapture is that it is a recent doctrine that was invented by John Nelson Darby in 1830, after being influenced by a young (and some claim, demonically possessed) woman named Margaret McDonald who supposedly had a vision about a pretrib rapture. I'm always a little surprised when I hear this argument because it has been so thoroughly debunked on every level. But it sounds somewhat intellectual and academic, so people keep presenting it as an argument.

However, with only some cursory research, people will find that the claim does not actually hold any water and is completely, historically incorrect. Proverbs 18:17 aptly states, "In a lawsuit the first to speak seems right, until someone comes forward and cross-examines." In this case, a very basic cross-examination quickly reveals the complete falsehood of this claim.

First, there are records showing Darby had started to formulate his understanding of the pretrib rapture at least three years beforehand, in 1827.[1] Second, Darby is not the first to recognize a pretrib rapture in Scripture. As I mentioned in the previous chapter, church fathers and theologians who held to an ancient pretrib view include figures as far back as Irenaeus (a student of Polycarp who was directly discipled by John).

Two experts, Drs. Ed Hindson and Mark Hitchcock, in their book cite various comments from additional early church fathers, including Clement of Rome (AD 35–101) and Ignatius of Antioch (d. AD 110), that show a belief that the Lord could return at any moment.[2] They also highlight several medieval period documents that demonstrate a belief in the pretrib view.[3] Here is one crystal-clear quote they include. It is taken from a sermon from Pseudo-Ephraem, a Syrian church father (fourth to seventh century). It reads, "We ought to understand thoroughly therefore, my brothers, what is imminent...and prepare ourselves for the meeting of the Lord Jesus Christ...For all the saints and elect of God are gathered together before the tribulation, which is to come, and are taken to the Lord."[4]

As highlighted in the previous chapter, from the fourth to sixteenth centuries the Catholic Church tightly controlled what was taught by the church. Eventually, only Latin Bibles were allowed, and these were often chained to the pulpit. So the average Christian did not have access to Scripture in their everyday language. The Protestant Reformation and the invention of the printing press changed all of that. When people began to read and study Scripture for themselves, they began once again to study eschatology—including the rapture.

From that point forward grew a steady stream of various theologians returning to a basic, yet unformalized, pretrib-premil view. Darby simply packaged the doctrine in a formalized way. It is important to note that detailed formalization of doctrines was not the norm prior to the Enlightenment period of the 1600s through the early 1800s, when the practice of carefully cataloging concepts to teach became popular. Universities and seminaries grew out of this era. Darby was well qualified to perform such a task with the doctrine of the rapture (along with dispensationalism). Furthermore, Darby was no quack. He was educated at Westminster School and Dublin's Trinity College. He was a lawyer, then a priest, then later, founded the Plymouth Brethren Church and wrote several books, including a Bible translation and a French-language overview of every book of the New Testament.[5]

Finally, it does not matter when a particular doctrine became popular. What matters is if it is in the Bible! For example, salvation by grace through faith was not a "popular" doctrine until the Reformation in the sixteenth century. Theologians would hardly agree that it is therefore wrong. The fact is this doctrine can be thoroughly backed up with Scripture. So the ten reasons to believe in the pretrib rapture that are below (after I address common argument number 2) are all taken directly from *the* authoritative source—the Bible!

On a related note, I have noticed that those who cite this argument (that Darby invented the concept of the pretrib rapture) also often refer to it as "the secret rapture doctrine." This secondary part of their argument seems to imply that those of us who hold to the pretrib position think it will happen in secret and go unnoticed.

But when millions of believers suddenly vanish, and millions more bodies in graves, morgues, and hospitals go missing, this event will hardly be a secret. Far from it. The post-rapture chaos will be the key domino that sets all other end-times events into motion. It will create the opportunity for the antichrist to emerge on the global stage, claiming that he will bring order to all the chaos.

Common Argument #2

The other common argument I often hear is that Christians are not immune to tribulation and should therefore expect to go through some or all of the tribulation period. Also, proponents of this argument often assert that those who hold to the pretrib rapture are escapists who want to avoid suffering for the Lord. This argument fails to understand the difference between general tribulation and *the* tribulation.

There is a difference between suffering and enduring the active wrath of God. Scripture is clear that believers will indeed face tribulation (John 15:18-25; 16:33; 2 Timothy 2:3; 3:10-13). *Tribulation* is another word for trouble, or suffering. As believers we are not spared from suffering or persecution (John 15:20). After all, we live in a fallen world that is heavily influenced by the schemes of our enemy (Ephesians 6:12; 1 Peter 5:8). We live in enemy territory. Satan is referred to as the "god of this age" (2 Corinthians 4:4) and the "prince of the power of the air" (Ephesians 2:2 NASB).

Right now, many of our brothers and sisters in Christ are being persecuted and martyred in various places around the globe. At the time of my writing this chapter, thousands of Christians in Nigeria have been killed and hundreds of thousands more have been displaced by jihadists who are waging war in north and central Nigeria. Seven thousand Christians have fled persecution in Syria in recent years, and 3 million Christians in Somalia are displaced due to persecution by al-Shabaab militants.[6]

We find additional persecution in North Korea, much of the Muslim world, and in various places in Asia. The first 300 years of the church saw barbaric waves of persecution throughout the Roman Empire, and there has been persecution in various areas of Christendom throughout the church age.

So, yes—Christians have, do, and will face tribulation. But there is a vast and undeniable difference between tribulation in general and *the* tribulation as a specific end-times period. The tribulation period (detailed in Revelation chapters 6–19) is not a general characteristic of a fallen world; it is a specific seven-year period (Daniel 9:27) of God's active and purposeful judgment upon the world (i.e., the Day of the Lord; Isaiah 2:12; 13:6-9; Joel 1:15;

2:1-31; 3:14; 1 Thessalonians 5:2) and his unfinished business with Israel and the Jewish people (i.e., the time of Jacob's trouble; Jeremiah 30:7).

With those two primary arguments addressed, let us now turn our attention to some clear biblical reasons to believe and teach the doctrine of the pre-trib rapture.

Top Ten Reasons to Believe in the Pretrib Rapture

These are my personal top ten reasons to believe in the pretrib rapture. By the way, if you would like to discover additional reasons, you may want to consult Dr. John Walvoord's thorough list of 50 reasons in his book *The Rapture Question*.[7]

Reason #1: The Seven-Year Tribulation Period Is Uniquely and Specifically for the Jewish People

Context is key, and the foundational framework for the tribulation period (and all things end times) comes from Daniel 9, which lays out all of Jewish history, including the fact that the final seven years of world history will refocus on the Jewish people. In other words, the main purpose of the future tribulation period is not focused on the church. Daniel 9:24 very clearly states that the entire 490-year prophetic time frame (including the final seven years of Daniel 9:27) is "for your [Daniel's] people [the Jewish people] and your holy city [Jerusalem]."

In Matthew 24, the words of Jesus support this Jewish focus as he highlights prophetic details of the end times, including the abomination of desolation in a temple in Jerusalem (verse 15), his advice to flee Judea at that time (verse 16), and his admonishment to pray that this future flight from Judea would not be on the sabbath (verse 20). Here in Jesus' great end-times teaching (the Olivet Discourse), his focus is clearly not on the church, but Israel, the Jewish people, Jerusalem, and the tribulation-era temple.

Reason #2: The Church Will Be Kept From (Not Through) the Tribulation Period

Revelation 3:10 clearly states that the church will be kept *from* (Greek word *ek*, meaning "out of," not "through") the hour of trial *that will come upon the whole earth*. The entire tribulation period is God's wrath. Jesus opens the seals, and by the sixth seal judgment, the inhabitants of earth clearly state they know they are experiencing God's wrath (Revelation 6:15-17).

Reason #3: The Church Is Completely Absent from the Judgments in Revelation

The word *church* is mentioned some 19 times in the first three chapters of Revelation but not mentioned at all during the entire description of the judgments described in chapters 6–19. The word *church* is only mentioned one more time, in Revelation 22. The people who become believers during the tribulation period are not referred to as the church, but simply as "saints" (Revelation 13:7 NASB). In Revelation 19, we see the symbolism of the church (dressed in fine linen) returning with the Lord as part of the armies of heaven. As further support, the lampstands—described by Jesus in Revelation 1 as representing the churches—appear in heaven in Revelation 4, along with the 24 elders who clearly represent the church (as shown by their crowns and white garments). This is after John is told to "come up here" (verse 1) and before the judgments begin in Revelation 6.

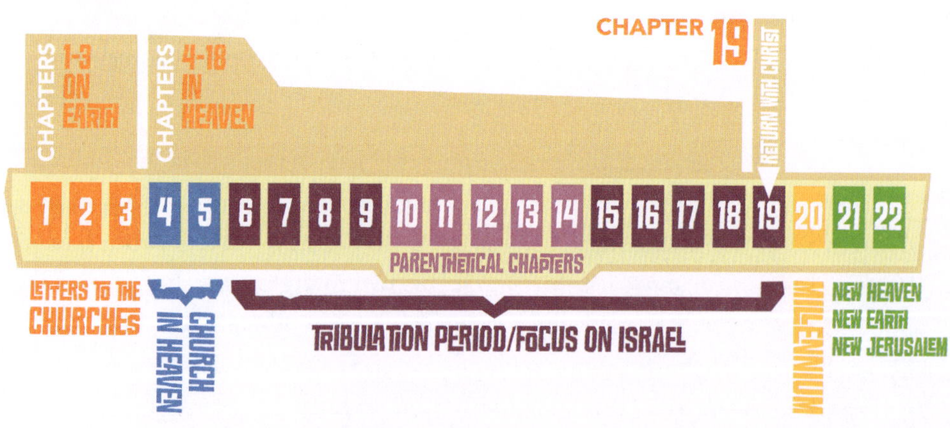

In place of the church, we learn about two witnesses from Jerusalem; 144,000 Jewish people (12,000 from each tribe of Israel); a vision of a woman clothed with the sun, moon, and 12 stars (a clear allusion to Joseph's dream from Genesis 37); and the armies of the world gathered in Israel to assemble for battle in the valley of Megiddo (Revelation 16:16).

Reason #4: Paul's Chronology of the Rapture Followed by the Day of the Lord

As highlighted earlier in this book, the most detailed passage of the rapture is found in 1 Thessalonians 4. Immediately following those key verses about the rapture (verses 13-18), Paul moves into a discussion of the Day of the Lord (5:1-5), which is another term for the seven-year tribulation period.

When introducing the new topic of the Day of the Lord, Paul used the Greek phrase *peri de*, which is translated "Now as to" (NASB). Paul always used this transition statement to introduce the next topic he addressed. One expert cites, "Paul uses this phrase eight times in his writings—twice in 1 Thessalonians (4:9; 5:1) and six times in 1 Corinthians (7:1, 25; 8:1; 12:1; 16:1, 12). In every instance, he uses it to introduce a new topic. Pay careful attention to Paul's order of topics in 1 Thessalonians. Christ comes to remove His church from the earth (chapter 4). New topic (*peri de*). Here's what will happen in the day of the Lord (chapter 5). The day of the Lord, a time of trouble, follows the rapture of the church."[8]

Reason #5: The Church Is Not Appointed to the Coming Time of Wrath

In the context of Paul's teaching about the Day of the Lord (God's active judgment upon the world) highlighted in Reason 4, Paul states in crystal-clear terms, "For God did not appoint us to suffer wrath but to receive salvation through our Lord Jesus Christ" (1 Thessalonians 5:9).

The context is very clear that Paul is not talking about God's eternal wrath (i.e., hell), but the time of wrath known as the future Day of the Lord. While we are saved spiritually when we accept Christ, our physical/final redemption is not complete until we receive our glorified bodies. Right now, we are "sealed for the day of redemption" (Ephesians 4:30), awaiting the resurrection/rapture.

By the way, 1 Thessalonians 5:9 is not an isolated verse. It reflects the pattern of Paul's teaching. In 1 Thessalonians 1:10 the apostle wrote, "To *wait for his Son from heaven*, whom he raised from the dead—Jesus, who rescues us *from the coming wrath*." Paul could not have been more clear.

Reason #6: The Doctrine of Imminency

The clearly taught doctrine in Scripture on this matter (see partial list below) is that the Lord could return at any time without any preconditions. This can only be true of the pretrib view. With any other view, there are necessary preconditions. We're not told anywhere in Scripture to look for the emergence of the antichrist, but instead, to "wait for his [God's] Son" (1 Thessalonians 1:10). As soon as the future antichrist officially confirms and completes a peace covenant between Israel and many nations, the tribulation period will begin. Only the pretrib view can support the doctrine of imminency, which is clearly taught throughout the New Testament.

IMMINENCY

- **PHILIPPIANS 3:20**
- **1 THESSALONIANS 1:10**
- **TITUS 2:13**
- **1 PETER 4:7**
- **REVELATION 22:7, 12, 20**

Reason #7: The Restrainer Must Be Removed Before the Antichrist Can Be Revealed

In 2 Thessalonians 2, where Paul was assuring the Thessalonians that they were not in the Day of the Lord already—as false teachers had told them (verse 2)—we learn some additional details that further support the pretrib rapture.

First, we are told that the Day of the Lord (i.e., tribulation period) cannot begin until there is a great apostasy (falling away from truth) and until the antichrist is revealed (verse 3). (Remember, it is important to note here that the rapture does not begin the tribulation period, but the confirming of the Daniel 9:27 covenant does.) Then we learn, in verses 6-8, that this revealing of the antichrist cannot happen until the restrainer is removed. The restrainer is referred to as both a *what* and a *he*. The restrainer is none other than the Holy Spirit-indwelled church. At the moment of the rapture, the salt and light influence that the church has on the earth will be removed. There will be no restraining the power of evil that will come crashing in on the world at the moment the church is removed.

The church age began on the day of Pentecost when the Holy Spirit was sent to dwell in believers. The church age will officially end when the Holy Spirit's indwelt influence is removed via the rapture. Now, the Holy Spirit is omnipresent and part of the Trinity. He will not cease his activity after the rapture. But his unique work that is being completed during the church age will come to an end when the church is taken to heaven.

So to recap the logic of this argument, fact 1 is that the tribulation period cannot begin until the antichrist is revealed. Fact 2 is that the antichrist cannot be revealed until the church is removed. Therefore, the logical and necessary chronology is that the rapture will occur first, then the antichrist will be revealed, and then the tribulation period will begin.

Reason #8: Comfort

Following Paul's detailed description of the future rapture in 1 Thessalonians 4, he concludes with a comforting statement in verse 18, "Therefore encourage one another with these words." The doctrine of the rapture is meant to encourage us, to comfort us, and to assure us that Jesus paid it all and that we get to escape the coming wrath of God on earth because of our security and position in Christ.

Titus 2:13 (discussed earlier in this book) even calls the rapture our "blessed hope." It is what we are looking forward to. Nowhere does Scripture tell Christians to prepare to endure hell on earth. Every mention of the Lord's return is painted as something we look forward to with joyous anticipation. During the tribulation, most believers—people who will have placed their faith in Christ after the rapture—will be martyred. That is not a "blessed hope." Nor is it a comforting thought for believers today.

Reason #9: God's Clear Pattern of Rescuing the Righteous Before Judgment Falls

Our Lord is a God of order, character, and consistency. While he is God and can do whatever he pleases, there is a pattern of predictability in Scripture when it comes to his redemptive work and his love for the righteous who place their faith in him. We discover a consistent pattern in Scripture where God always rescues his people before his active wrath is unleashed. We see this clear pattern in the biblical record in how God dealt with Enoch, Noah, and Lot. In each case, the righteous were physically removed prior to God's judgment. As we'll see in an upcoming chapter, Enoch was literally raptured—caught up to heaven (Genesis 5:24) prior to judgment. Noah and his family were protected and lifted above the judgment (Genesis 7). Lot was physically

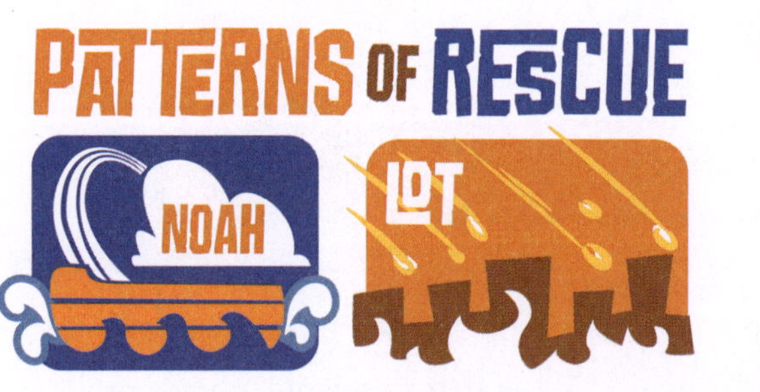

taken out of the city by angels before God's judgment fell on Sodom and Gomorrah (Genesis 19:16).

Reason #10: The Clear Symbolism of Ancient Jewish Wedding Customs in Scripture

The bride waited eagerly. Her excitement grew because she knew her groom would show up soon—with his best man announcing their sudden arrival. She hadn't seen him since their engagement. She knew the time for his arrival was nearing, and her anticipation swelled with each passing day.

The groom's father paid a great price—the *mohar*—for her hand in marriage. Because the bride's family was losing a vital member of their household, this custom seemed only fair. The couple's engagement was a legally binding event. It wasn't a question of *if* her groom would come for her; it was only a question of *when*.

Back at the father's house, his son was hard at work, building an addition for his future bride. The father observed carefully as his son lovingly crafted the new living quarters. It would initially serve as the honeymoon suite—to be enjoyed for the traditional seven days after the wedding ceremony. The father thoughtfully estimated the time needed for everything to be perfectly ready. He set a date in his mind. And only he knew the exact day he would send his son to go fetch his bride.

At the house of the bride, those who were carefully watching events unfold knew the arrival of the groom could happen at any moment. Knowing that the time for this momentous event was drawing near, the bride readied herself. Bags packed.

Wedding dress on. Lamp filled with oil. Wick lit. Hugs given. Tears of joy and life-transition shed. One night passed, and no groom. But it had to be close. Then another. Still, no groom. And another. Just when she thought she could wait no longer, it happened!

A trumpet and a shout from the best man to the bride broke the night's silence from the far side of the family field. The bride rushed out to see. *Could this be it? Is this really happening?* she thought. By the time she reached the field, the few who were watching went out to join the celebration and witness the sudden snatching away of the bride. Her groom swept her into his arms and looked her in the eyes. "Never again will we be apart," he whispered. "Come, let me show you what I have made for you."

Ancient Jewish wedding traditions portray a clear type or picture of the rapture. God the Father paid the *mohar*. He gave his "only begotten" Son as the payment for our sins (John 3:16 NASB1995). The church is known in the New Testament as the bride of Christ. Jesus said he was going to "prepare a place" for us (John 14:3). He has been preparing this place for his bride for 2,000 years. Many who were watching have fallen asleep. The promised return of the Groom eventually became a myth in their minds.

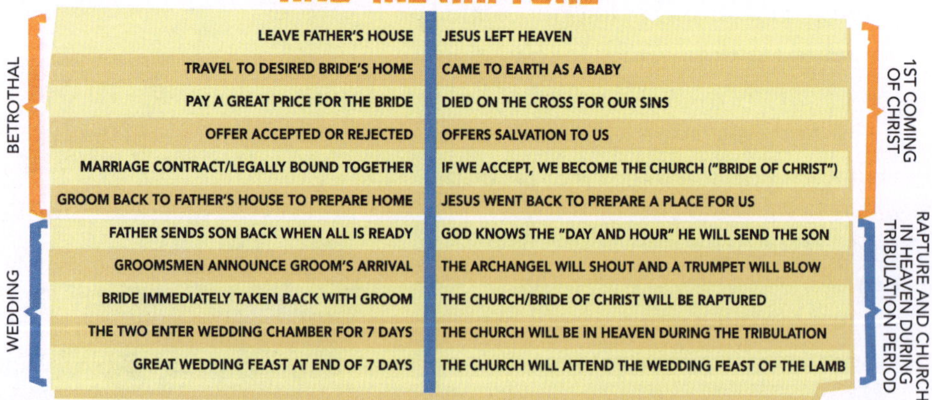

JEWISH WEDDING TRADITIONS AND THE RAPTURE

	Jewish Wedding Tradition	The Rapture	
BETROTHAL	LEAVE FATHER'S HOUSE	JESUS LEFT HEAVEN	1ST COMING OF CHRIST
	TRAVEL TO DESIRED BRIDE'S HOME	CAME TO EARTH AS A BABY	
	PAY A GREAT PRICE FOR THE BRIDE	DIED ON THE CROSS FOR OUR SINS	
	OFFER ACCEPTED OR REJECTED	OFFERS SALVATION TO US	
	MARRIAGE CONTRACT/LEGALLY BOUND TOGETHER	IF WE ACCEPT, WE BECOME THE CHURCH ("BRIDE OF CHRIST")	
	GROOM BACK TO FATHER'S HOUSE TO PREPARE HOME	JESUS WENT BACK TO PREPARE A PLACE FOR US	
WEDDING	FATHER SENDS SON BACK WHEN ALL IS READY	GOD KNOWS THE "DAY AND HOUR" HE WILL SEND THE SON	RAPTURE AND CHURCH IN HEAVEN DURING TRIBULATION PERIOD
	GROOMSMEN ANNOUNCE GROOM'S ARRIVAL	THE ARCHANGEL WILL SHOUT AND A TRUMPET WILL BLOW	
	BRIDE IMMEDIATELY TAKEN BACK WITH GROOM	THE CHURCH/BRIDE OF CHRIST WILL BE RAPTURED	
	THE TWO ENTER WEDDING CHAMBER FOR 7 DAYS	THE CHURCH WILL BE IN HEAVEN DURING THE TRIBULATION	
	GREAT WEDDING FEAST AT END OF 7 DAYS	THE CHURCH WILL ATTEND THE WEDDING FEAST OF THE LAMB	

All the symbolism related to the two advents of the Messiah mirrors these ancient Jewish wedding traditions. If you will recall from our earlier discussion about John 14:1-3, I highlighted how Jesus often used that rich tradition as an illustration in his teachings. In the ancient Jewish marriage custom, the groom would leave his father's house, travel to the desired bride's home, pay a great price for the bride, have his offer accepted or rejected, become legally bound if his offer was accepted, and then go back to his father's house to prepare a place for his bride.

At a specific time known only to the groom's father, the son would be sent to go get his bride. The groomsmen would announce the groom's arrival, then the bride would be lifted onto a special seat to be carried away with the groom. The couple would enter the wedding chamber for seven days, and then there would be a great wedding feast after the marriage was consummated.

Nowhere in that symbolism is there any room, rhyme, or reason for the beloved bride to suffer any amount of wrath from the father before she is good enough for the son. The bride does not have to be purified (as some assert) to enter heaven. Jesus paid it all on the cross. He said, "It is finished" (John 19:30). If we think we can bring anything to the table to make ourselves *more pure* (a redundant term) than we are when Christ's righteousness has been imputed to us at salvation, then we have a critical misunderstanding of God's grace and the very doctrines of sin and salvation.

I'll admit that, as a man, I do not readily relate to the excitement of a bride waiting for her groom. But I do fully relate to the excitement of waiting to be with someone I love. Years ago, for a whole year, my wife and I dated long distance before we got engaged—her in Arkansas and me in Maryland. Then, we were engaged for another year before we got married. I can still remember the excitement as I waited for the back doors of the church to open and for my soon-to-be wife to emerge as everyone turned their attention to her as she walked down the aisle.

Right now, at this very moment in history, we have more reason than any other generation to believe that the rapture of the church is close. As we trust the Lord, plan our lives, and continue living out our days, we should do so with the excitement and anticipation of a bride on her wedding day or a groom waiting for those church doors to open, so the beloved can finally be together.

It Has Legs!

So as you can see by now, the pretribulational rapture is not a doctrine developed from an individual's personal feelings, selfish hopes to escape tough times, the false visions of a 15-year-old demonized girl, or wishful theologians infusing their own ideas into Scripture. The pretrib view has stable legs and can withstand the attempts to shake its foundation. The testimony of Scripture and church history bear out the veracity of this solid, clear-cut doctrine.

For those of us who are convinced of and waiting for the pretrib rapture, just when we think we can no longer wait—perhaps very soon—the Father will send the Son to fetch his bride.

SECTION 2:

THE BACKSTORY

THE HISTORY AND BROADER CONTEXT

Raptures in the Old Testament

Enoch walked faithfully with God; then he was no more, because God took him away.

GENESIS 5:24

Have you ever wondered why the square that boxers contend in is called a ring? Shouldn't it be called a square? Ever wonder why the boxing ring is covered in canvas? Or ever wonder why championship bouts are limited to 12 rounds? These and other facets of modern boxing have their roots in the years of trial and error in the sport, and the need for standardization.

In the eighteenth century and early nineteenth century, boxing was fought bare-knuckle and took place in a roughly drawn circle on the ground. Under the feet of the fighters was the simple dirt floor or the bare ground of wherever the contest was set to take place. In 1743, the London Prize Ring rules dictated that a small circle be placed in the middle of the fight space, where the two opponents would meet at the beginning of each round. The first square-shaped fighting space was introduced by the Pugilistic Society in 1838, but the term *ring* had already stuck. At this point, it was less about the shape and more about the space. In 1853, the rules were modified and included a standard that the "ring" would be a 24 foot by 24 foot square made on turf. [1]

Over time, the need for an elevated platform developed so that a larger audience could view the contests—and more event tickets could be sold—which became the norm. Along with that, the need for a durable, stretchable, nonslip surface that could soak up blood, sweat, and water was needed. This led to the common use of canvas to overlay the surface of the ring.

Boxing also used to have an unlimited number of rounds. There is no need for scorecards or judges if the fighters contend until one of them simply cannot continue. The only downside for the organizers is that people get bored and fewer tickets are sold. Not to mention the long-term damage suffered by the fighters subjecting their bodies and brains to such long bouts.

The longest recorded boxing match took place on April 6, 1893. A fight between Andy Bowen from New Orleans and Jack Burke from Texas went 110 rounds and lasted seven hours and 19 minutes. It started at 9:15 p.m. and lasted until 4:34 a.m. After such a long bout, it was stopped and declared a *no contest* (and later, officially changed to a draw).[2]

The history of modern boxing helps us to see why certain details have become standards in the sport. These older milestones of standardization help make sense of the sport today—and can hint at where the sport is headed in the future. But few people know a lot about these earlier examples of boxing.

Similarly, people often assume the only rapture in the Bible is the yet-future rapture of the church as described in the key text of

1 Thessalonians 4. In fact, there are at least seven additional raptures that are recorded in Scripture. In this chapter, we will survey the Old Testament to discover the first two raptures recorded in the Bible, and we'll also look at a few other interesting Old Testament passages as well.

Enoch

Enoch is a surprisingly popular figure in Scripture, though few people know much about him. He is mentioned six times in Genesis, once in 1 Chronicles 1:3, and an additional three times in the New Testament (Luke 3:37; Hebrews 11:5; Jude 14). If you haven't heard of Enoch, perhaps you have heard of his son, Methuselah—who happens to have been Noah's grandfather.

In Genesis 5, we learn that Enoch was 65 when Methuselah was born (verse 21), and then, he lived another 300 years (verses 22-23). If you are wondering how people lived for so long back in the patriarchal era, the main reason (I believe) is that the corruption of sin and decay in the human body, as well as the environment, became progressively worse over time. Genesis 3 calls it the curse. Science caught up a few thousand years later during the nineteenth century's scientific age and refers to it as the second law of thermodynamics—also known as the law of increasing entropy (decay/energy loss).

Over time, the effects of mankind's fall have taken their toll on every aspect of existence, including the average lifespan. That's a topic for another book, but I wanted to mention it here because I know some readers will be curious. Now, back to our regularly scheduled topic.

After receiving the basics about Enoch's genealogy, we are given this single mysterious statement in Genesis 5:24, where we read, "Enoch walked faithfully with God; then he was no more, because God took him away."

Enoch walked with God. This implies closeness. Intimacy. In Genesis 3:8, we find Adam and Eve hiding from God, who was "walking in the garden in the cool of the day." This seems to have been their regular fellowship based on the question God posed when Adam and Eve were hiding—"Where are you?" (Genesis 3:9). Even today in the church age, we refer to our relationship with the Lord as walking with him. It is a term of closeness and of heading in the same direction.

Enoch didn't walk away from, apart from, or in opposition to the Lord. He walked "with" the Lord. It is of note that this phrase was only used of Enoch (Genesis 5:22, 24) and Noah (Genesis 6:9). Enoch and Noah loved and obeyed the Lord. They walked in close fellowship with him.

In contrast to the other family members listed in the Genesis 5 genealogy, Enoch did not die—he was taken. The most literal translation of Genesis 5:24 is found in the NASB which reads, "Enoch walked with God; and he was not, for God took him." The word "took" here is *laqach* in Hebrew, and according to *Strong's Concordance* it means "to take," "capture," "carry," "seize," or "take away."[3] Everywhere the word is used in Genesis it is translated as some form of the phrase *taken away*—physically moved to another location.

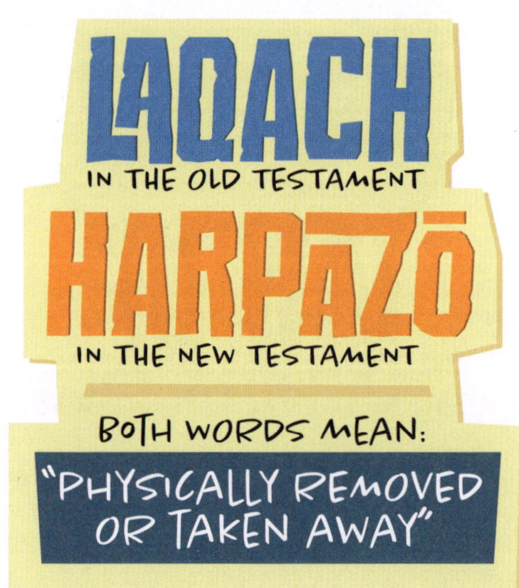

If God took Enoch, the only logical conclusion is that he was taken to be with God in heaven. Jude 14 mentions Enoch's knowledge about the coming of the Lord with "thousands upon thousands of his holy ones." Compare that with the description of the Lord's return in Revelation 19. Verse 14 informs us that "the armies of heaven were following him, riding on white horses and dressed in fine linen, white and clean." So Enoch—who walked closely with the Lord—was given insight into how it would all end with the Lord's victorious arrival!

If there were any doubt that Enoch escaped death by way of a rapture, we read the following in Hebrews 11—the great Faith Hall of Fame:

> By faith Enoch was taken from this life, so that he did not experience death: "He could not be found, because God had taken him away." For before he was taken, he was commended as one who pleased God. And without faith it is impossible to please God, because anyone who comes to him must believe that he exists and that he rewards those who earnestly seek him (verses 5-6).

Last, but not least, please do not miss the fact that Enoch was taken before the global judgment of the flood (Genesis 6–7). As mentioned in the previous chapter, God's pattern of judgment is that he physically removes the righteous prior to bringing judgment.

Elijah

Elijah stands as the key representative of the prophets from the Old Testament. He lived during the ninth century BC and shows up out of nowhere in the pages of Scripture. All that we are told is that he was from an area called Tishbe from the northern kingdom of Israel (1 Kings 17:1). Elijah mentored another man who would take over the mantle of prophet from him. This man's name was Elisha (1 Kings 19:19), and Elijah literally threw his mantle on him as a symbolic gesture. The two were very close and ministered together training other prophets.

Just as mysteriously as Elijah showed up on the scene, he exits. Without any preamble or explanation as to how the prophets knew what was about to happen, we read the following in 2 Kings 2:1-3:

When the LORD was about to take Elijah up to heaven in a whirlwind, Elijah and Elisha were on their way from Gilgal. Elijah said to Elisha, "Stay here; the LORD has sent me to Bethel." But Elisha said, "As surely as the LORD lives and as you live, I will not leave you." So they went down to Bethel. The company of the prophets at Bethel came out to Elisha and asked, "Do you know that the LORD is going to take your master from you today?" "Yes, I know," Elisha replied, "so be quiet."

Then again, in verse 5, another group of prophets from Jericho say the same thing to Elisha and get the same response. So the entire school of the prophets knew Elijah was about to be taken.

Then, we read this a few verses later:

> As they were walking along and talking together, suddenly a chariot of fire and horses of fire appeared and separated the two of them, and Elijah went up to heaven in a whirlwind. Elisha saw this and cried out, "My father! My father! The chariots and horsemen of Israel!" And Elisha saw him no more. Then he took hold of his garment and tore it in two (verses 11-12).

I find it very interesting that the two examples of raptures in the Old Testament seem to display two key purposes of the rapture. Enoch was taken before God's judgment came. Elijah was taken (apparently) because his assignment was finished, his calling was completed, and he was rewarded for his life of faithful service to the Lord.

Another important detail regarding Elijah is that Scripture has foretold that he will once again step onto the world scene, just before the tribulation period is set to begin. Malachi 4:5-6 predicts, "See, I will send the prophet Elijah to you before that great and dreadful day of the LORD comes. He will turn the hearts of the parents to their children, and the hearts of the children to their parents; or else I will come and strike the land with total destruction."

Even today, Jewish seders held during Passover include an empty chair at the table in anticipation that Elijah will return to usher in the Messiah in fulfillment of Malachi's prophecy. Most don't realize it will be the Messiah's second advent. And sadly, many of them will accept a false messiah first—the antichrist who will confirm a covenant with Israel and many (Daniel 9:27).

I believe Elijah will be one of the two witnesses of Revelation 11:3-12. We discover them in the parenthetical chapters of Revelation connected to key midpoint events at around the three-and-a-half-year mark of this future time of God's wrath. But the signs they perform mirror Moses and Elijah, and in fulfillment of Malachi's prophecy, Elijah will appear before the tribulation begins. I believe he will enter the scene after the rapture and before the confirming of the Daniel 9:27 covenant.

John the Baptist came in the spirit and power of Elijah (Luke 1:17). John was the last of the prophets, in the mold of Elijah—even down to his clothes and his challenges to the rulers of his day. But Jesus affirmed that the complete fulfillment of Malachi's prophecy was still yet future (Matthew 17:11).

Daniel Chapter 8

While Enoch and Elijah are the only people actually raptured in the Old Testament (where God physically took them to heaven without dying), there

are a few other interesting events that I would like to share in preparation for some of the New Testament rapture accounts we will consider in the next chapter.

In chapter 8 of the book of Daniel, the prophet Daniel recorded a vision he had. In the vision he saw himself in Susa, the capital of Persia in the province of Elam (in modern-day southern Iran, just north of the Persian Gulf). Note a difference here. Daniel wasn't taken to Susa, but in the vision he saw himself in Susa. Daniel's vision was a prophecy of the future indicating he would outlive the Babylonian Empire and find himself in the heart of the Persian Empire. So this was not a rapture, but a vision of Daniel seeing himself somewhere else. I have heard it referred to as a rapture, but a careful look at the text reveals Daniel simply saw himself in the vision but was not actually relocated there.

Ezekiel Chapter 8

Ezekiel's case seems to be slightly different than Daniel's. While Daniel saw himself in a vision, Ezekiel states he was spiritually transported to Jerusalem (Ezekiel 8:1-3) in a vision. The text reads,

> In the sixth year, in the sixth month on the fifth day, while I was sitting in my house and the elders of Judah were sitting before me, the hand of the Sovereign Lord came on me there. I looked, and I saw a figure like that of a man. From what appeared to be his waist down he was like fire, and from there up his appearance was as bright as glowing metal. He stretched out what looked like a hand and took me by the hair of my head. The Spirit lifted me up between earth and heaven and in visions of God he took me to Jerusalem, to the entrance of the north gate of the inner court, where the idol that provokes to jealousy stood.

In Daniel's case, he saw himself at another location. In Elijah's case, he seems to have been spiritually, or possibly physically, transported to another location. Keep these two accounts in mind as we consider the first-century raptures covered in the next chapter.

Understanding the Past

Just as we can better understand the terminology, rules, and traditions of modern-day boxing by studying the history and backstory of the sport, so too can we fully grasp the doctrine of the rapture when considering the full counsel of God and dissect these key accounts in the Old Testament. Everything in the New Testament is built upon the foundation of the Old Testament. So with that foundation set, let us turn our attention to the raptures of the first century!

Chapter 6: Raptures in the First Century

She gave birth to a son, a male child, who "will rule all the nations with an iron scepter." And her child was snatched up to God and to his throne.

REVELATION 12:5

Regulated boxing is nearly ubiquitous internationally. It is a standard sport in the Olympics and enjoys a united amateur system in the United States and most other countries of the world. There are rules and governing bodies for amateur and professional boxing on the local, regional, national, and international levels. Standardization of various rules and details has allowed the sport to gain international traction and served to help the sport thrive. Fighters know what to expect in their participation, so they can focus on building their amateur or professional career.

Standardization helps pave the way from a pugilist's first amateur match, to their first professional match, and beyond. Clarity in the early details provides insight and a well-defined path in each step toward a boxer's long-term vision and goals.

When it comes to the rapture, the key text descriptions of the ultimate future event (John 14:1-3; 1 Corinthians 15:52; 1 Thessalonians 4:13-18) are not the only examples of raptures we can learn from in the pages of Scripture. In the previous chapter, we considered the raptures of the Old Testament. Now, we turn our attention to the first-century raptures that occurred and are recorded for us to study.

Seven raptures are recorded for us in the New Testament, but two of them reference the same event—so technically, there are six New Testament raptures. Four of them occurred in the first century. They were experienced by Jesus, Philip, Paul, and John.

So while we may be familiar with the texts describing the fully developed standardized version of the future rapture of the church, there are other first-century rapture events recorded in the pages of the New Testament. One happened prior to the church age (Jesus' ascension), and three others occurred in the early days of the church age, after the Holy Spirit descended on the day of Pentecost. There is much we can learn from these other accounts. Most notably, they further support the clear teaching of the main rapture event that the church has been waiting for, for the past two millennia.

Jesus

In Acts 1:9-11 (cf. Luke 24:51), we read about Jesus' ascension. There we read, "After he said this, he was taken up before their very eyes, and a cloud hid him from their sight. They were looking intently up into the sky as he was going, when suddenly two men dressed in white stood beside them. 'Men of Galilee,' they said, 'why do you stand here looking into the sky? This same Jesus, who has been taken from you into heaven, will come back in the same way you have seen him go into heaven.'"

Remember that Luke and Acts are two volumes of the same book, so to speak. Luke wrote his Gospel as a careful record of the life of Christ (Luke 1:3) and he wrote the book of Acts (addressed to the same individual—Theophilus) to record the birth and expansion of the early church.

In John 16:7, Jesus mentioned to his disciples that he could not send the Holy Spirit unless he himself returned to heaven. The ascension of Jesus from the Mount of Olives was the fulfillment of this prophecy. Notice the passage from Acts 1 also mentions that Jesus will return in the same way in which he left. Not only in the same way, but Zechariah 14:4 states that he will return to the same exact place—the Mount of Olives!

We also notice some key details related to Jesus' rapture. As with the account at the Mount of Transfiguration, where three of his disciples witnessed Jesus in his glory as Moses and Elijah appeared (Matthew 17:5; Mark 9:7; Luke 9:34-35), and as with the prophecies of Christ's future return to earth at the end of the tribulation period (Matthew 24:30; Mark 13:26; Luke 21:27), we discover that the glorious and mysterious clouds of heaven are present at the ascension as well. These three important markers—the transfiguration, the ascension, and the physical return of Christ—are three markers in the same divine sequence of events.

The second reference to Christ's ascension is found in Revelation 12, where we learn about a vision John had of a great sign in the sky. In the first five verses, we read:

> A great sign appeared in heaven: a woman clothed with the sun, with the moon under her feet and a crown of twelve stars on her head. She was pregnant and cried out in pain as she was about to give birth. Then another sign appeared in heaven: an enormous red dragon with seven heads and ten horns and seven crowns on its heads. Its tail swept a third of the stars out of the sky and flung

> them to the earth. The dragon stood in front of the woman who was about to give birth, so that it might devour her child the moment he was born. She gave birth to a son, a male child, who "will rule all the nations with an iron scepter." And her child was snatched up to God and to his throne (verses 1-5).

The Woman

This woman with the sun, moon, and 12 stars represents Israel. In Genesis 37:9-11, we read about Joseph's dream, which uses the same symbolism of the sun, moon, and stars. Joseph was one of the 12 sons of Jacob (whose name was changed by God to Israel), and these 12 sons were the official leaders of the 12 tribes of Israel. A careful study of Scripture leads us to the solid conclusion that this woman symbolizes Israel who brought forth (i.e., gave birth to) the Messiah—Jesus. Which leads us to the next character. During the second half of the tribulation period, Israel will flee into the desert where God will protect them for 1,260 days (or three and a half years).

The Male Child

The male child represents Jesus. Through Israel, God brought us the Scriptures and the Savior. Jesus is Jewish to the core—the Lion of the Tribe of Judah (one of the 12 sons of Israel), the descendant of David who will one day "rule all the nations with a rod of iron" (Revelation 12:5 NASB). Jesus completed his earthly mission and ascended into heaven's throne room. Here, in

Revelation 12, is where we get confirmation that the ascension of Christ was indeed a rapture. The phrase "snatched up" is our now-familiar word, *harpazō.*

The Dragon

The enormous red dragon represents Satan. This chief fallen angel has attempted to thwart the Messiah's arrival through various means—but has failed every time. Satan's cosmic rebellion along with one-third of the angels got them all kicked out of heaven and hurled down to the earth.

Notice in this passage from Revelation 12 that Jesus was "snatched up" to heaven (verse 5). This term in Greek is our now-familiar word, *harpazō*. So, in Acts 1 and Revelation 12, we have two accounts of the same event—the special rapture of the Messiah, known to most as the ascension.

Philip

In Acts 8, we encounter our next rapture of the first century, and this one is quite different. Unlike Enoch, Elijah, or Jesus, who were taken to heaven, Philip was raptured instantly to another area known as Ashdod, some 20 miles away from his original location (Acts 8:39-40). Philip was one of the original deacons appointed by the church in Jerusalem (Acts 6:1-7), had taken part in powerful and effective ministry in Samaria (Acts 8:1-8), and was led by an angel to Gaza (Acts 8:26) in the extreme southwestern area of modern-day Israel—an area known all too well after the horrific attack on innocent civilians in southern Israel on October 7, 2023, initiated from within what is known as the Gaza Strip.

Prophecy experts Hindson and Hitchcock note two important details about the account of Philip:

> First, it took place by the Spirit of the Lord, the Holy Spirit. This is the first mention of the third Person of the Trinity being involved in a rapture event. Certainly Father, Son, and Spirit will be involved in the future rapture of all believers. Second, the passage notes that after the baptism, "the eunuch no longer saw Philip." Though

Philip was only temporarily raptured to another location, this event highlights an important aspect of the future rapture of the church: Those who remain on earth will no longer see those who were raptured.[1]

I'd like to point out one other detail we observe from Philip's rapture. The moment Philip's work of leading the Ethiopian eunuch to the Lord and into the waters of baptism was completed, Philip was raptured away. Similarly, once the work of the church is done, the bride will be whisked away to heaven. Once the full number of church-age Gentiles are saved, God will shift his focus back to Israel (Romans 11:25-27). Only God knows when that moment will be, so we must work hard until we are called home via death or rapture. Jesus' parable in Luke 19:11-27 reminds us to work hard investing in kingdom purposes until he comes back.

Paul

In 2 Corinthians 12:1-4, we read the following words from the apostle Paul, who referred to himself in third person (not out of arrogance but to make a point), "I must go on boasting. Although there is nothing to be gained, I will go on to visions and revelations from the Lord. I know a man in Christ who fourteen years ago was caught up to the third heaven. Whether it was in the body or out of the body I do not know—God knows. And I know that this man—whether in the body or apart from the body I do not know, but God knows—was caught up to paradise and heard inexpressible things, things that no one is permitted to tell."

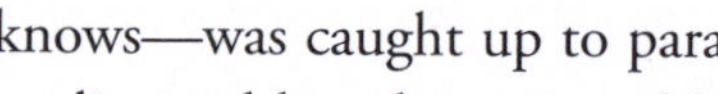

Paul shared more about his personal life and ministry challenges in 2 Corinthians than in any of his other letters. He did so in response to critics who were challenging his apostolic authority and claiming equal authority with the apostle (10:1–13:10). So the apostle's hand was forced in a sense, and he laid out his apostolic credentials as a last-ditch effort to get the church in Corinth fully back on track in terms of recognizing legitimate authoritative direction from the Lord.

In this revealing letter, Paul shares that he was caught up (*harpazō*) to heaven and was immediately in the presence of the Lord. He was brought there for the express purpose of receiving heavenly intel. Presumably, this was when Paul learned of several mysteries, including the mystery of the rapture (1 Corinthians 15:51-52).

John

The apostle John was banished to the Isle of Patmos where he received divine revelation to write the book that shares the same name, Revelation. After receiving the seven letters from Jesus to the churches of Asia Minor (located in modern-day Turkey) in chapters 2–3, we read this in the two opening verses of Revelation 4:

> After this I looked, and there before me was a door standing open in heaven. And the voice I had first heard speaking to me like a trumpet said, "Come up here, and I will show you what must take place after this." At once I was in the Spirit, and there before me was a throne in heaven with someone sitting on it.

The word *harpazō* is not used in this account, but the details line up with what we know about the rapture. John sees an open door in heaven, hears a voice like a trumpet, and is told to "come up here." We do not know exactly what we will see or what phrase will be uttered at the moment of the rapture, but we do know we will hear a loud command, the voice of an archangel, and a heavenly trumpet blast (1 Thessalonians 4:16). Do you have goose bumps yet? Just wait until chapter 7!

JOHN

What Can We Learn?

We can learn much by analyzing these first-century rapture accounts. Second Timothy 3:16 reminds us that "all Scripture is God-breathed and is useful for teaching, rebuking, correcting and training in righteousness." All Scripture is inspired and intentional. Every detail is important and purposeful. These rapture accounts provide precedent for the rapture of the church. Here are a few key takeaways that we can garner from these accounts:

- We can expect to be immediately in the presence of the Lord once raptured.
- We can expect to see, hear, and feel inexpressible things a millisecond after the rapture.
- We can expect the rapture to take place the moment the work of the church is done on earth.
- Like Philip, once we are raptured, those left behind will see us no more.
- Like Paul, we will be in paradise.
- Like John, we will see the Lord in his glorified form—sovereignly ruling.

If you know the Lord, let those details renew your mind and uplift your spirit. Lift your gaze to heaven's throne room and remind yourself often that one day every struggle will be left behind!

If you do not know the Lord, today is the day of salvation. Respond to the gift that God has secured for any who would bow their knee to Jesus and accept him as Savior, so that you will not be left behind to face the deception and horrors of the tribulation period. Every breath is a gift, and we are not guaranteed our next one. Choose Christ today. Come to the Messiah who literally gave his life for you. If you are being drawn into a relationship with Christ, pause here and go read chapter 16!

As we consider these past raptures in the Old and New Testaments, we should take note that the synthesis of Scripture supports two key theological concepts—the inspiration of Scripture and the doctrine of the rapture.

The fact that various raptures are found in Scripture—from Enoch and Elijah, to Paul and John, to the church and the two witnesses of Revelation (discussed in the next chapter)—shows the divine hand of a single Author. Furthermore, when one carefully studies the details of all the rapture accounts throughout the Bible, they fully support the overall doctrine of the rapture of the church and its importance in God's redemptive plan. The rapture is not some minimally important teaching or fabricated doctrine. It is interwoven into the full biblical narrative. With those two thoughts as the backdrop, and with the various rapture accounts serving as the proverbial boxing undercard, now it is time for the main event!

CHAPTER 7

Raptures in the Future

God did not appoint us to suffer wrath but to receive salvation through our Lord Jesus Christ.

1 THESSALONIANS 5:9

Every fight card consists of several matches. First, there are what are known as undercard bouts. These are the up-and-comers, the first-time professional fighters, and the prospects—those who are working their way up to prize-fight level, who show promise of becoming a household name, and who help build anticipation and excitement for the main event.

The early fights on a card are usually not well attended. The audience is thin and usually only those who know the two contenders personally are there to support their respective corners. First-time professional fighters usually fight four rounds that are three minutes each. This is one round more than their amateur experience has them conditioned for. As the schedule works its way up through the card, the boxers are more experienced and the bouts are longer—six-, eight-, then ten-round bouts all make up the undercard of a major boxing event. With each bout, the stadium or event center becomes increasingly full of people, noise, and anticipation.

Finally, the moment arrives when it is time for the main event—the championship bout that everyone in attendance or watching on TV paid to witness. The 12-round championship bout is full of all the drama and spectacle of a Rocky film—complete with entrance songs for each fighter and an extensive well-crafted introduction by the ring announcer. Just before the bout begins, the ring announcer captures the crowd's attention, and after a pregnant pause, proclaims, "Ladies and gentlemen, this is the moment you've all been waiting for!"

Divine D-Day

Now that we have navigated our way through the raptures of the Old Testament and the first century—the undercard, if you will—it is time for the main event! Despite what some current voices are saying, the imminent rapture of the church is *the* key moment that believers have been anticipating for nearly 2,000 years. The early church lived with the healthy expectancy of the Lord's "any-moment" return. We can study the interesting details of the undercard rapture accounts, but now—ladies and gentlemen of the church—this is the moment we've all been waiting for!

Our "blessed hope" (Titus 2:13) is designed to encourage and sustain us as we navigate our way through what Paul refers to as a "crooked and perverse generation" (Philippians 2:15 NASB). We are to encourage one another with the doctrine of the rapture (1 Thessalonians 4:18), and we are to remain occupied until the Lord returns (Luke 19:13).

The two contenders are Jesus—who longs to be with his bride—and Satan, who is the god of this age, the prince of the power of the air, and the dragon who constantly goes after the elect. Satan is not Jesus' equal—he is a created being, a fallen chief angel who is so self-deceived he thinks he can beat God.

For nearly two millennia, our adversary has tried at every turn to persecute the church. And for much longer than that, he has tried to destroy God's chosen Jewish people. But he has failed. The rapture of the church (and God's subsequent pivot of attention back to save the Jewish remnant) will be the culmination of church-age believers' salvation and another massive failure by the enemy to keep God's prophetic plans from fulfillment. To put it bluntly, believers are caught in an age-old spiritual war.

There are several details from 1 Thessalonians 4:16-18 (the Bible's primary rapture text) that are related to spiritual warfare. There we read of a "loud command," the "voice of the archangel," and the "trumpet call of God." When you carefully study these details in light of Scripture, they all have connotations of warfare. In the Old Testament, the shofar blast was used for many occasions, including the gathering of the assembly to move out and the gathering of the army to do battle. Archangels are seen as contending with the enemy in the supernatural realm (Daniel 10:13; Jude 9).

This makes sense when you consider the fact that Satan is described as: the prince of the power of the air (Ephesians 2:2); the god of this age (2 Corinthians 4:4); the ruler of this world (John 14:30); the ruler of the kingdoms of this world (Matthew 4:8); and, the deceiver of the whole world (Revelation 12:9). As a result of the fall, earth has been title-deeded to Satan. The future rapture of the church will be a heavenly special-ops snatch-and-grab invasion of enemy territory.

Notice that this seminal future event will take place in the clouds—right in the middle of the enemy territory of the prince of the power of the air. At the moment of the rapture, the spiritual warfare in the heavenly realm will invade our physical world unlike any other time in history. The current scientific theories of naturalism and uniformitarianism will be shattered in an instant when millions of Christians supernaturally disappear from earth via the *harpazō*.

This event will be like a divine D-Day. It will be a game-changing spiritual warfare campaign initiated by God himself, and it will set a whole series of events in motion—culminating in the utter defeat of enemy forces. Much like D-Day, the enemy knows this initial event is coming soon. He just doesn't know exactly when.

Unlike D-Day, the winning side will not experience any casualties. On the contrary, we will be more alive than we have ever been. The sacrifice has already been made by Jesus. Our spiritual salvation has been won. The D-Day–like rapture will complete the promise as our physical bodies are transformed to match our born-again spirits. "Therefore encourage one another with these words" (1 Thessalonians 4:18).

The second act of the two-part spiritual war campaign will occur at the end of the tribulation period, when Jesus leads "the armies of heaven" (Revelation 19:14) in an all-out invasion to defeat the enemy and physically reclaim the earth. By the way, if you are currently a believer in Christ, you have

been officially enlisted in the Revelation 19:14 armies of heaven! Those returning with Christ are described as wearing the same pure white church clothes that the church representatives in Revelation 4 were wearing when John was raptured up to witness heaven's throne room. The church will go to heaven before the tribulation begins (Revelation 6) and will return with the glorified Messiah at the end of the tribulation period as seen in Revelation 19!

What About the Old Testament and Tribulation Saints?

To briefly pivot back to our boxing analogy regarding the main event—in some super-bouts, there exists a newer phenomenon known as the co-main event. This occurs when there are two championship bouts on the same card. Well, as it pertains to the rapture, there is one more prophesied future rapture—the two witnesses of Revelation. And there's another major resurrection event—the resurrection of the Old Testament and tribulation period saints. Both will be highlighted in this chapter about future raptures and resurrections.

The Rapture of the Two Witnesses

In Revelation 11, we discover two strange end-times figures known as the two witnesses. They are also called the two olive trees and the two lampstands. We find a veiled reference to these figures in Zechariah 4:11-14, where Zechariah had to push for an answer as to who they were. He did not receive a full answer other than the confirmation they were indeed two individuals. Revelation 11:4 is a direct reference to Zechariah 4:14. Both passages reference the lampstands, olive trees, and state in which these figures stand before the Lord of the earth.

We are told that the witnesses will prophesy for 1,260 days—which comes out to three and a half years (using the Jewish 360-day year). We are told that they can breathe fire and destroy people who try to harm them, turn off the rain, turn water into blood, and strike the earth "with every kind of plague as often as they want" (Revelation 11:6). These end-times superheroes will undoubtedly capture the attention of the world during the first three and a half years of the tribulation period.

It seems that their ministry location is in Jerusalem where, at the midpoint of the tribulation, they are killed by the antichrist (referred to as the beast) to everyone's surprise and delight. In Revelation 11:9-10, we read, "For three and a half days some from every people, tribe, language and nation will gaze on their bodies and refuse them burial. The inhabitants of the earth will gloat over them and will celebrate by sending each other gifts, because these two prophets had tormented those who live on the earth."

Upon the death of the two witnesses, the world erupts into joy and initiates a new holiday tradition as they celebrate by sending gifts to one another to commemorate the antichrist's victory over these two disruptive fire-breathing preachers. But, just as the global celebrations get into full swing, God will throw a resurrection-sized monkey wrench into their party.

As was the case with the resurrection of Christ, this future resurrection of the two witnesses will surprise the enemy as the world learns that what they thought was a victory was actually a back-breaking defeat. In Revelation 11:11-13, we read,

> After the three and a half days the breath of life from God entered them, and they stood on their feet, and terror struck those who saw them. Then they heard a loud voice from heaven saying to them, "Come up here." And they went up to heaven in a cloud, while their enemies looked on. At that very hour there was a severe earthquake and a tenth of the city collapsed. Seven thousand people were killed in the earthquake, and the survivors were terrified and gave glory to the God of heaven.

Reminiscent of the rapture of the church, which will occur three and a half years prior to this event, we find this event with the two witnesses. Also note that they will hear the same direction John heard in Revelation 4, when he saw a door open to heaven's throne room and heard the command to "come up here."

The Identity of the Two Witnesses

While I cannot be dogmatic, I believe the two witnesses are Moses and Elijah, and I will explain why. Those two key Old Testament figures traditionally represent the law and the prophets (i.e., the entire Old Testament) and the tribulation period has a distinctly Jewish focus. Once the church is removed via the rapture, God's attention will turn back to the Jewish people during the tribulation period. Moses and Elijah also appeared at the Mount of Transfiguration (Matthew 17:1-13), when Jesus was seen in his glory by the three disciples Peter, James, and John.

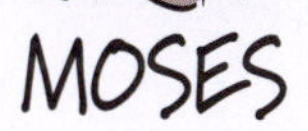

In Matthew 17:1-3, we read, "After six days Jesus took with him Peter, James and John the brother of James, and led them up a high mountain by themselves. There he was transfigured before them. His face shone like the sun, and his clothes became as white as the light. Just then there appeared before them Moses and Elijah, talking with Jesus."

Additionally, the miraculous signs the two witnesses are able to perform mirror those of Moses and Elijah, and their means of exiting the scene in the Old Testament were both very unique. Moses died and was buried by God himself (Deuteronomy 34) under very mysterious circumstances where Satan attempted to take the body of Moses (Jude 9). Elijah, on the other hand, was taken up to heaven without dying via a tornado-driven team of fiery horses (2 Kings 2:11-12).

Not all prophecy experts agree that the two witnesses will be Moses and Elijah, or even that they will be men that will be known from Scripture. Other popular candidates for who these individuals might be are John (the writer of Revelation) and Enoch.

In any case, I believe the ministry of the two witnesses will begin after the rapture and that Revelation 11 is describing the events related to the two witnesses that occur at the midpoint of the tribulation. There is a prophecy in Malachi 4:5-6 that states, "See, I will send the prophet Elijah to you *before that great and dreadful day of the LORD* [the tribulation period] comes. He will turn the hearts of the parents to their children, and the hearts of the children to their parents; or else *I will come and strike the land with total destruction*."

Based on this prophecy and the details described above, it appears that Elijah will most likely show up on the scene soon after the rapture, but before the official beginning of the tribulation period, when the antichrist is revealed by enforcing Israel's "covenant with many" (Daniel 9:27). John the baptizer came *in the spirit of Elijah* (Luke 1:17) before Jesus' first-coming ministry began, but Elijah himself will enter the scene in the end times, right before the tribulation period begins. Jesus affirms this two-fold fulfillment of Elijah's end-times ministry in Matthew 17:10-13.

The Old Testament and Tribulation Saints

In the opening section of Daniel 12, we are given a clear description of the tribulation period (and its clear focus on the Jewish people). In verses 1-4, we read,

> At that time Michael, the great prince who protects your people, will arise. There will be a time of distress such as has not happened

> from the beginning of nations until then. But at that time your people—everyone whose name is found written in the book—will be delivered. Multitudes who sleep in the dust of the earth will awake: some to everlasting life, others to shame and everlasting contempt. Those who are wise will shine like the brightness of the heavens, and those who lead many to righteousness, like the stars for ever and ever. But you, Daniel, roll up and seal the words of the scroll until the time of the end. Many will go here and there to increase knowledge.

Then, a few verses later in the same chapter, we read, "As for you, go your way till the end. You will rest, and then at the end of the days you will rise to receive your allotted inheritance" (Daniel 12:13).

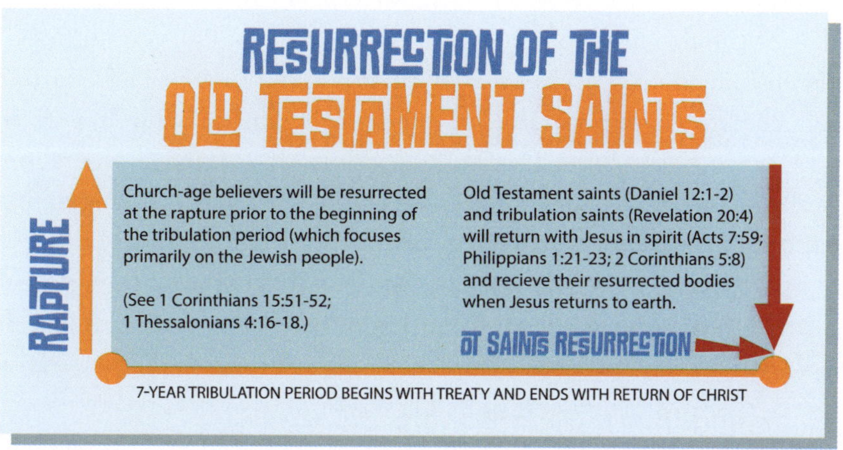

There is so much that we can glean from these passages, including the fact that the archangel Michael is tasked specifically with protecting the Jewish people. Think of the many times in Israel's modern history when they have been protected from repeated attempts by surrounding nations to wipe her off the map. Perhaps Michael is currently active, protecting the regathered Jewish people. It is certain that during the tribulation period, Michael will be active on the highest level possible—first protecting the 144,000, then after the midpoint of the tribulation period, supernaturally protecting a remnant of Jewish people in Bozrah, which is modern-day Petra in southern Jordan (see Isaiah 63:1 and Revelation 12:6-9).

After the rapture—at least for a time—there will be no believers on earth. For the first time in history there will not be a single righteous person on the planet! The restrainer will be gone (2 Thessalonians 2:6-8), the metaphorical levy will break, and a tidal wave of evil will crash in on the world to initiate the worst time period in all of history.

But the largest revival in history will also take place at that time. First, the two witnesses will enter the scene leading to the salvation of 144,000 Jewish young men. These first-fruit witnesses (along with resources and our witness left behind) will lead multitudes to faith in Jesus. Sadly, most of them will be martyred for their faith (see Revelation 6:9-11; 7:9-17; 13:7, 15-17; 17:6; 19:1-2).

These tribulation-era believers will be resurrected at Christ's return (at the very end of the tribulation period) to reign with the Lord for 1,000 years during the millennial kingdom (Revelation 20:4, 6). It is at this time that all Old Testament believers will be resurrected to receive their glorified bodies as well (see Job 19:25-27; Isaiah 26:19; Daniel 12:1-2; Hosea 13:14). Finally, there must logically be one final resurrection at the end of the millennial kingdom for those believers who are born during that time (the descendants of those survivors of the tribulation who will enter the kingdom in their natural bodies), or these future believers will receive their glorified bodies as soon as they die.

Anticipating the Co-Main Events

When anticipating boxing matches consisting of co-main events, fans are often torn over which match they want to see most. But within short order they get to witness both contests with equal excitement. As church-age believers, we are understandably most excited to witness (and experience) the first co-main event—the rapture. But we will also be greatly anticipating the resurrection of Old Testament and tribulation saints to enter the future millennial kingdom!

Saints from every era await the resurrection. First, the church via the rapture, which will officially end the church age. Then, the Old Testament and tribulation period saints at the end of Daniel's seventieth week, when Christ returns and "all Israel" (Romans 11:26) is saved (Zechariah 12:10-14; Matthew 23:39; Luke 19:42; Romans 11:25-32).

God in his sovereignty has a perfect plan to bring history and prophecy to an ultimate conclusion. Saints from all ages who have died are with the Lord in spirit, awaiting the redemption of their bodies. The promises of God to Old Testament saints, church-age saints, and tribulation period saints will be fulfilled in the two phases of the Lord's return. The Old Testament promises and the Old Testament resurrection brackets the New Testament church age in perfect symmetry—as you would expect from our Creator who is a God of beauty, mystery, design, and order.

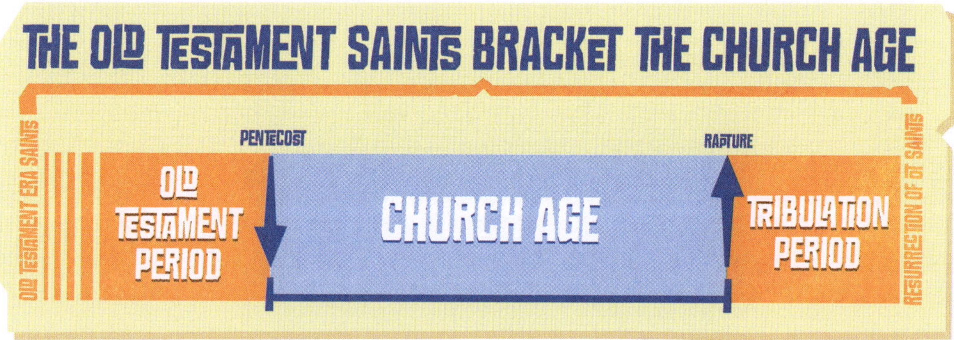

Only our almighty, triune God could orchestrate the events of world history to align perfectly with his prophetic word and bring all things to their perfect conclusion. The resurrection of Christ guarantees the future resurrection of all believers to receive their glorified bodies fit for heaven and eternity. What an amazing God we serve!

The Resurrection to Avoid

Multitudes who sleep in the dust of the earth will awake: some to everlasting life, others to shame and everlasting contempt.

DANIEL 12:2

In the boxing world, there are sanctioned and unsanctioned events. What this means is that one, or several, of the official governing bodies of boxing (known as alphabet soup because there are several of them now, as highlighted in chapter 3) oversee the rules surrounding the entire event. The WBA, WBC, IBF, and/or the WBO (depending on what championship belts are involved) have the legal obligation to ensure the safety of the competitors, verify the credentials of the ringside doctor and judges, and organize the process of weigh-ins, hand-taping, and the nutrition/supplement guidelines (including drug testing) for the entire card.

If fighters take part in an unsanctioned event, they are putting themselves at great risk with no real recourse should something go wrong with any of those areas of oversight listed above. In short, they are taking their life and livelihood into their own hands. Add to this the fact that their match will not even count on their official record. Simply stated, the risk and potentially negative outcome of such an event is all on the shoulders of the boxer who chooses to take part in an event apart from an official governing body.

Well, when it comes to resurrections, you most definitely want to be part of a sanctioned event—one that is governed by the official governing authority of heaven and earth. To take part in the officially sanctioned resurrection you need to be clothed in the righteousness of Christ. When we stand before God, we either stand in our own sinful state or we stand in imputed holiness via the shed blood of the Lord Jesus Christ.

We learn what God did for us in 2 Corinthians 5:21, where we read, "He made Him who knew no sin to be sin in our behalf, so that we might become the righteousness of God in Him" (NASB). Those of us who have placed our faith in the Messiah had our sin placed on the cross. Sanctioned or unsanctioned. Those are the only two possibilities.

In Revelation 20:6, we read, "Blessed and holy are those who share in the first resurrection. The second death has no power over them, but they will be priests of God and of Christ and will reign with him for a thousand years."

Though there are multiple raptures and resurrections as detailed in previous chapters, they are all part of the first resurrection—the resurrection to eternal life. The first type of resurrection is the one you want to be a part of. The second type of resurrection is most definitely not the one you want to experience. If you are reading this and realize that you would stand before God based on your life instead of the perfect sinless life of Christ, feel free to pause here and go directly to chapter 16 to discover exactly how to receive Christ as your Savior to be a part of all future sanctioned events!

THE TWO TYPES OF RESURRECTIONS

TYPE 1: BELIEVER'S RESURRECTION
TYPE 2: UNBELIEVER'S RESURRECTION

So there are two types of events. Or as Daniel and Jesus highlight for us—two types of resurrections. Jesus elaborated on the two types of resurrections that Daniel recorded for us in the verse at the opening of this chapter.

In John 5:25-29, Jesus taught,

> Very truly I tell you, a time is coming and has now come when the dead will hear the voice of the Son of God and those who hear will live. For as the Father has life in himself, so he has granted the Son also to have life in himself. And he has given him authority to judge because he is the Son of Man. Do not be amazed at this, for a time is coming when all who are in their graves will hear his voice and come out—those who have done what is good will rise to live, and those who have done what is evil will rise to be condemned.

Like any good teacher, Jesus leaves out the complexity of the various raptures and resurrections and simply highlights the two *types* of resurrections—one to receive eternal life and the other to receive condemnation. The structure of the sentence even hints at the fact that the two types of resurrections will be separated as different events.

All the unbelieving dead have been awaiting judgment in what Jesus refers to in Luke 16:28 as the "place of torment." Technically speaking, it is a compartment in what Scripture calls *Hades* in the New Testament (Luke 16:23) or *Sheol* (the grave/realm of the dead) in the Old Testament. It is not the final state of the unrighteous. It is essentially a spiritual holding tank where they await the final judgment.

In modern terms, it is similar to how a person remains in jail while awaiting trial. Then, if found guilty, after the trial's sentencing, the prisoner is moved from a temporary county jail to their final sentence in a state prison. Hades is like a county jail, and the lake of fire will be like a maximum-security state prison. I unpack the progressive revelation of the afterlife in greater detail in my book *The Non-Prophet's Guide™ to Spiritual Warfare*.

We learn the details about the second resurrection in Revelation 20, which apparently takes place after the conclusion of the millennial kingdom, Satan's last stand, and the purging of the current heavens and earth (see 2 Peter 3:10 and Revelation 20:11). It is known as the great white throne judgment—and it is the final, single judgment for all unbelievers over all of time.

Of all the passages of Scripture, Revelation 20:11-15 is the one that scares me the most. Not because it applies to me, but because it applies to anyone. Imagine the moment when God's only recourse is to be fair. That may not sound scary, but it is. Throughout history, God has offered grace, mercy, and forgiveness. In fact, he went so far as to die a tortuous death and experience the wrath of the Father in our place so we could avoid getting what we deserve.

Here is what I mean. We either get what is fair—and must pay for our own sins—or we receive God's grace and forgiveness. But grace and forgiveness are only found if we accept his gracious offer. The cross is the scandal of the ages. Who else lets people off the hook and pays the price for it with their very own life? Or harder yet, the life of their one and only beloved Son! Yet many people reject this offer of forgiveness. Jesus himself warns us in Matthew 7:13-14, where he succinctly and bluntly stated, "Enter through the narrow gate; for the gate is wide and the way is broad that leads to destruction, and there are many who enter through it. For the gate is narrow and the way is constricted that leads to life, and there are few who find it" (NASB).

I don't know all the intricacies of how, when, and why people are responsible for rejecting Christ, but God does. And after every possible avenue is exhausted to give people time to repent and turn to Christ, the inevitable must come.

After the millennial kingdom, the final rebellion, and Satan's ultimate judgment, we read about a future event where all unbelievers will stand before God to answer for their sins. Keep in mind that this is literally the last event of history before the permanent and perfect eternal state commences.

We read about this future event in Revelation 20:11-15, where John describes what he saw with these words,

> Then I saw a great white throne and him who was seated on it. The earth and the heavens fled from his presence, and there was no place for them. And I saw the dead, great and small, standing before the throne, and books were opened. Another book was opened, which is the book of life. The dead were judged according to what they had done as recorded in the books. The sea gave up the dead that were in it, and death and Hades gave up the dead that were in them, and each person was judged according to what they had done. Then death and Hades were thrown into the lake of fire. The lake of fire is the second death. Anyone whose name was not found written in the book of life was thrown into the lake of fire.

In this amazing scene we see everything literally fade away except the throne and the books. Are these literal books or some kind of heavenly databank? The word used here for books is *biblos* (βίβλος) and it means a sacred or supernatural scroll, book, or volume. It is a supernaturally kept volume of data on each person who has ever lived.

If you think the data centers that governments and transnational data companies have are big, think about the amount of data God has kept! Every thought, action, motive, and word of every person who has ever existed has been kept in God's supernatural library of "books."

Also notice that John mentions that the lake of fire is the second death. In Scripture, we learn that there are two births and two deaths. There is a natural birth when we were physically born, and there is a potential spiritual birth if we accept Christ (John 3:3-6). There is a natural death when our current physical bodies die, and there is a second spiritual death, which John refers to as the lake of fire. So if you are born twice, you die once, but if you are born once, you die twice.

And as highlighted above, there are also two resurrections. What Scripture ultimately reveals is that there are two types of resurrections—a believers' resurrection and an unbelievers' resurrection. As noted, there are multiple believers' resurrections, but only one unbelievers' resurrection—described by John in Revelation 20.

Levels of Punishment in Hell

The existence of hell is a tough pill to swallow, but we must submit our sin-laced thinking to the authority of Scripture and the character and sovereignty of God. When we compare our sinfulness to the absolute holiness of God, there is no room to argue.

In one of my seminary courses we studied the book of Romans in depth. One of the exercises was to study the holiness of God for an entire week through readings, exegetical studies, and lectures. Then the following week, we took the same approach to the nature of sin in general and our own sin nature specifically.

Today, I am probably more spiritually mature than I have ever been in my life—but the juxtaposition of the holiness of God and my own sinfulness hit me like a ton of bricks. Soaking in the holiness of God for a week helped me see my own sin nature like I hadn't seen in a long time. It helped remind me that it was not simply sin in general that put Jesus on the cross. It was *my* sin that put Jesus on the cross. Not simply my past sin or my worst moments, but my sin now in my current walk with the Lord.

More was broken by the fall than we even realize. Humans cannot even imagine what life without sin and a sin nature will be like. We do not realize how sinful we are in our fallen bodies and in this fallen world any more than a fish understands how wet it is in the ocean. This is why the doctrine of hell seems so extreme to us in our fallen nature.

C.S. Lewis is noted for stating that if there were one doctrine he would like to ignore or eliminate, it is the doctrine of hell.[1] Yet, we cannot. It is included in the Canon of Scripture and Jesus taught on the topic more than anyone else in the Bible (see Matthew 5:22; 8:8-12; 18:9; 23:33; 25:41; Mark 9:43). We simply cannot fathom the immense distance between the holiness of God and the sinfulness of mankind.

Yet we can take some comfort in God's character and perfect justice. Just as there will be degrees of reward in heaven (via the *bema seat/judgment seat of Christ*), there will be degrees of punishment in hell. Luke 12:42-48 describes varying degrees of punishment symbolized by either many or few lashes. To be blunt, Hitler will suffer far worse than the average lost soul in hell.

FOR FURTHER STUDY...

on the topic of punishment degrees see:

John 19:11-12; Hebrews 10:28-29; 2 Peter 2:20-22

Carefully notice the last four words in this passage in Revelation 20:12-13, where we read, "I saw the dead, the great and the small, standing before the throne, and books were opened; and another book was opened, which is the book of life; and the dead were judged from the things which were written in the books, *according to their deeds*" (NASB).

OUR SINS + THE CROSS = RECONCILIATION WITH GOD

According to their deeds. One thing we always need to keep in mind when considering eternal punishment is that God is 100-percent fair in his dealings. Someone must pay for our sins because we can't get right with God on our own. Jesus paid the penalty and offers us the most amazing gift ever given. It is free to us, but it cost him everything.

If we reject God's offer to pay our sin debt, then we are 100-percent fairly judged based on our specific actions while we lived. Unfortunately, if we want separation from Christ in this life, he has no choice but to answer that prayer in the afterlife. The truest definition of hell is complete separation from God.

Just Juxtaposition

The extreme contrast between a sanctioned and unsanctioned boxing event demonstrates, on a microlevel, the polar-opposite eternal condition of those who take part in the two types of resurrections. Here's the beauty, we each have a choice as to which resurrection we are going to take part in. This is a limited time offer. We're not guaranteed another day, and Scripture implores us to act fast. There is a principle in the Bible that human beings should respond to the drawing of the Holy Spirit today. For example, Isaiah 55:6 reads, "Seek the LORD while he may be found; call on him while he is near." And Psalm 95:7-8 reads, "Today, if you will hear His voice, do not harden your hearts" (NASB).

We don't want to be like the rich young ruler who was so close to salvation but refused to cross the line of faith because of his love of money. We don't want to be like Pontius Pilate who had *the* Truth standing in front of him when he asked the jaded question, "What is truth?" (John 18:38). We don't want to be like Pharaoh or the future tribulation-period "earth-dwellers" who first harden their own hearts only to have them hardened more by the Lord himself.

Here's your call to action if you do not know the Lord: Make sure you take part in the first resurrection! And here is your call to action if you do know the Lord: Be intentional about inviting others to take part in the first resurrection!

Rapture Chronology

When the set time had fully come, God sent his Son.

GALATIANS 4:4

When planning for a championship fight, a boxer's training is very specific and carefully crafted to beat a specific opponent. Each component of the plan has a specific purpose and is often detailed in a training manual or fight camp strategy. When it comes to boxing, there is a logical chronology of events in a training camp.

Once contracts are signed, the date and location of the fight are chosen, and the coaching team goes to work putting together the schedule and specific goals for training camp—all designed to achieve victory. First, an assessment of the potential weaknesses of the opponent is made. The specific styles of the opposing fighters are considered. Hours of footage from previous fights of both competitors are analyzed. Finally, a detailed training plan is crafted to prepare the athlete for the impending match.

Training camp can be anywhere from 6–16 weeks for championship bouts (depending on how much notice is given and what condition the fighters are already in). This focused period of rigorous training is designed to provide the boxer with the maximum probability of winning the bout.

Training camp involves intensified conditioning through running, shadowboxing, bag training, mitt training, jumping rope, core strengthening, and additional strength and conditioning exercises. The coach and fighter work on specific techniques to be used for the match at hand. Once the strategy is formed and the specific techniques are refined, sparring is added to the training regimen.

The coaching team usually hires hand picked sparring partners that mirror the style, size, and capabilities of the upcoming opponent. The goal is to help their fighter be as ready as possible to face the opposing fighter of the impending bout.

So as to not risk injury by sparring or over-training, a week or so before the bout sparring ceases, but moderate conditioning and technique training continue. The goal is to maintain peak conditioning, while allowing the body to rest and heal. A few days from the bout, all training stops and the fighter focuses on obtaining maximum rest—particularly for the final two or three days before the match.

Similarly, most major prophetic fulfillments do not occur in a vacuum. The stage must be set first through a logical order of events. Pertaining to the first coming of Christ, we are told that he came in "the fullness of the time" (Galatians 4:4 NASB). Aside from God's sovereign decrees surely coming to pass, this also means that the conditions had to be readied. The table had to be set. In the case of the first incarnation, the Roman road and seafaring systems had to be in place so that when persecution began in Jerusalem, the gospel could be spread in the rest of the known world. Similarly, the common Greek language known as Koine Greek had to be ubiquitous in the ancient world for the good news of Jesus Christ to be shared far and wide. All these puzzle pieces along with God's foreordained prophetic timing had to come together.

In previous chapters we have considered the various views and the overwhelming strength of the pretribulational view of the rapture and the premillennial view of the Lord's return. We arrived there by using the only consistent hermeneutic known as the literal method for studying Bible prophecy. Literal, meaning all fulfilled prophecy was literally fulfilled, so we conclude that all yet-future prophecy will also be literally fulfilled and that the literal meaning of all texts must be synthesized to come to a conclusion about eschatological details.

In this chapter, I want to briefly unpack the basic order of all end-times events that can be logically placed on a timeline, along with their relationship to the timing and nature of the rapture. Just as the pieces of the puzzle had to come together for the first coming, so the stage must be set for the events of the second coming.

Speaking of puzzle pieces, that is what we piece together when we study the pages of Scripture to assemble the timeline of the end times. While certain things can be known easily through a verse or two—broader systematic theology of any sort must synthesize all related verses to put the puzzle together. This is by design. Salvation is simple enough a child can understand, but systematic theology takes quite a bit more work.

Church history contains the record of how various lines of theology were developed and put into creeds to help define orthodox theology. This was usually in response to heretical views that arose at different times. For example, the foundational doctrine of the Trinity was developed over a period of a few hundred years in response to various heresies related to the roles and nature of the three members of the Godhead—Father, Son, and Holy Spirit.

One of the class requirements in my seminary was the "History of Doctrine." In that class, we went through church history (from the first-century ancient church through the postmodern church of today) seven times—one for each major area of doctrine. They are as follows:

SEVEN MAJOR AREAS OF DOCTRINE

- The Doctrine of the Scriptures—Bibliology
- The Doctrine of God—Theology Proper
- The Doctrine of Christ, the Person of Christ—Christology
- The Doctrine of Christ, the Work of Christ—Christology
- The Doctrine of Salvation—Hamartiology, Anthropology, and Soteriology
- The Doctrine of the Church—Ecclesiology
- The Doctrine of Last Things—Eschatology

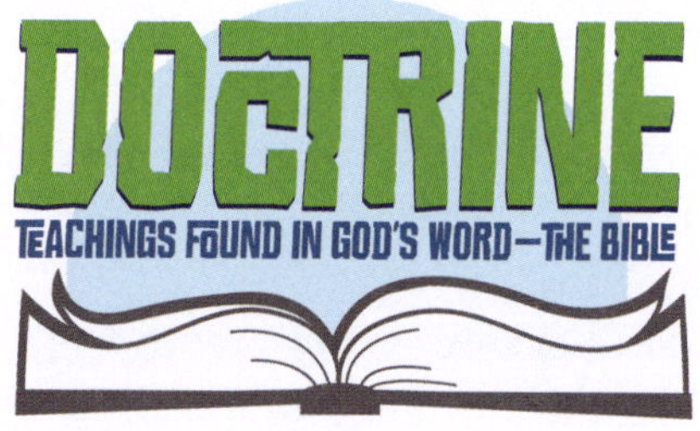

As you can see from that list, each major area of doctrine takes great consideration and careful attention to the entire Bible. You put the puzzle pieces together carefully, considering how they fit with all the other relevant pieces.

Using that analogy, I would like to share the puzzle pieces of eschatology to show how a logical, necessary timeline can be assembled with complete biblical integrity. Let's dump the puzzle pieces on the table and begin to piece them together!

Assembling the Major Puzzle Pieces

The Day of the Lord

The first big puzzle piece is the Day of the Lord. This is a major theme of the Old and New Testaments and refers to a specific time period when God will judge the nations for the purpose of settling accounts at a point and time toward the end of history.

Generally speaking, the Day of the Lord is any time God sends a specific prophesied judgment to a group of people—as he did with both Israel and

Judah for their disobedience and idol worship. God warned them in Deuteronomy 28 (among other places) that their obedience would bring blessing and that disobedience would bring judgment.

However, more broadly speaking, the Day of the Lord refers to a specific prophesied end-times judgment. Context lets the reader know which way the term is used. Often, a prophet would speak about the immediate context of impending judgment for Israel or Judah, then would transition into prophecies regarding the yet-future Day of the Lord at the end of the age. In the New Testament, this theme is picked up and always refers to the Day of the Lord, which will come upon the entire world.

I should also note here that when it comes to the eschatological or end-times Day of the Lord, sometimes the reference is to the time of judgment (the tribulation period), and sometimes the reference is to the ultimate result of the Day of the Lord—the kingdom. The judgment of the world through the 21 judgments in Revelation and the return of the Lord to destroy the armies of the antichrist serve as the necessary process to usher in the millennial kingdom. As always, context is key. The context determines which aspect of the Day of the Lord is in view.

When it comes to Scripture in general and Bible prophecy specifically, there is a term known as *progressive revelation*. What this means is that as we move through the pages of Scripture, we learn certain details that are usually a bit vague at first, but then we are given more information as we move chronologically through the story of the Bible. Progressive revelation functions like a work of art that begins with a loose sketch and ends with a fully rendered detailed masterpiece. Another analogy is that of entering a dark room that has a light with a dimmer switch that is slowly brought up over time, bringing the room from complete darkness to full illumination.

Well, in Daniel 9 we read such progressive revelation as we are given the actual duration of the Day of the Lord. In Daniel 9:27, we are told that the antichrist (referred to in Daniel 9:26 as "the prince who is to come" [NASB]) will broker a peace covenant between Israel and "many" for seven years. Then, this evil ruler who fools the world into thinking he is a peacemaker will break the covenant and turn on Israel halfway through the seven-year period. Jesus refers to this future traitorous event in Matthew 24:15 as "the abomination that causes desolation" and affirms it is the very event "spoken of through the prophet Daniel."

In the final book of the Bible, we are provided with more specifics about the judgments that will occur in the future Day of the Lord. In Revelation 6–19, we discover 21 specific judgments, several key mid-tribulation period events, and additional broad characteristics of the Day of the Lord.

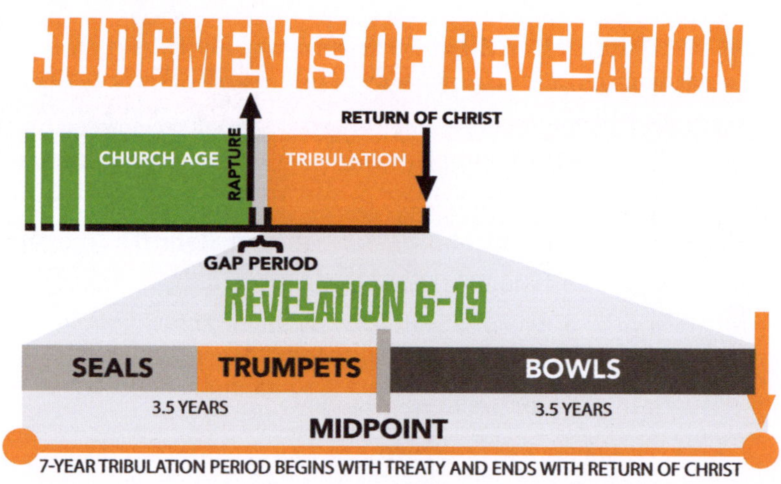

As highlighted in earlier chapters, the church age began with the arrival of the Holy Spirit on the day of Pentecost, and it will conclude with the removal of the Holy Spirit via the rapture, and this event can occur at any moment. It is an imminent event. The chaos of the world after the rapture will provide the perfect scenario for the full emergence of a one-world government, the revealing of the antichrist, and the confirmation of the Daniel 9 covenant, which will officially begin the future tribulation period.

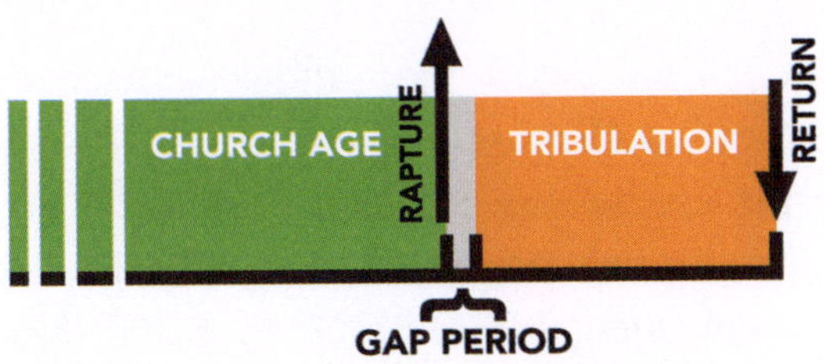

The Kingdom Age

The next big puzzle piece is the future kingdom age. As with the Day of the Lord, the kingdom age is also a major theme of the Old and New Testaments. In fact, in some contexts the Day of the Lord includes the kingdom age because one leads logically to the other. The purpose of the Day of the Lord is to settle accounts with the nations who have rebelled and to set up God's perfect kingdom on earth.

While it can be tempting to conclude that this future glorious kingdom age is mere allegory, the prophetic details are too specific, and we are given no indication in the text that these details should be taken any other way but literally. Where poetic language or symbolism is used in Scripture, it is clear what the poetic language or symbols represent. But when it comes to the future kingdom age, we are provided with many specific details about people, animals, the nature and topography of the world, and the future worldwide government with a descendant of David ruling from Jerusalem.

One detail we are not provided with until the very end of the Bible is the duration of this future golden age. In Revelation 20, we are told six times in as many verses that this future kingdom era will last 1,000 years. Again, there is no hint that this time frame should be taken in any way but literally. It is even repeated six times to drive this point home. Church-age believers will rule and reign with Christ, making his name known across the earth. At the end of this time, Satan will be released for one final deception and battle. He will quickly be defeated, and then thrown into the lake of fire, where he will remain permanently (Revelation 20:7-10).

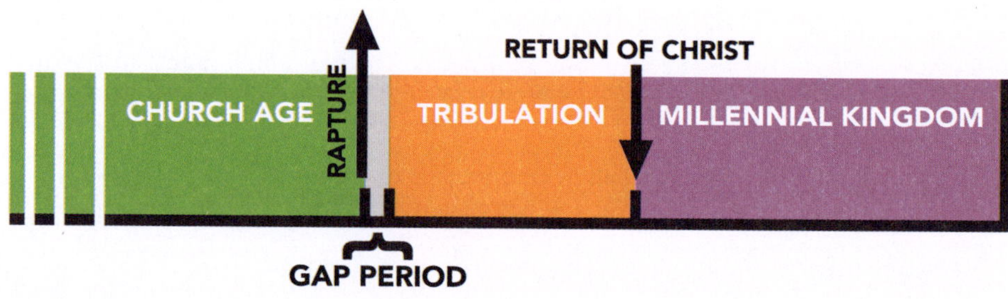

The Great White Throne Judgment

After Satan is cast into the lake of fire, there will be an unbelievers' judgment (detailed in chapter 8). At this judgment, all the nonbelievers from throughout history will stand before God to be judged, and sadly, cast into the lake of fire (Revelation 20:11-15). Believers will not stand before God at this judgment because their sins have been covered by the atonement of Jesus. Likely, believers will be residing in their custom-built living spaces in the new Jerusalem during this judgment, and also during the final event on our timeline.

The New Heaven and New Earth

All of creation will be completely renovated or recreated. Everything will be restored! The center of activity and God's presence will be in the new Jerusalem, but we will presumably be able to spend eternity traveling the vast expanse of heaven.

Assembling the Other Puzzle Pieces

With the major puzzle pieces described above all in place, there are other puzzle pieces that fall in place as well. I wanted to cover the large puzzle pieces first. And with that foundation, here are a few more pieces to further complete the picture.

The Judgment Seat of Christ

I believe that immediately following the rapture will be the judgment seat of Christ, also known as the bema seat. This is where we as church-age believers will receive an evaluation of our work for Christ after our salvation. It is where we will receive eternal rewards for use in the kingdom and beyond. Various crowns are mentioned, and other rewards include varying levels of responsibility as we rule and reign with Christ. Among the final words of Jesus recorded for us in Scripture are, "Look, I am coming soon! My reward is with me" (Revelation 22:12).

The Marriage

The mystical union of Christ and the church will be formalized. Our longing to be with Christ and his longing to be with the church will finally be an official and permanent reality. This will all happen with much fanfare and celebration.

The 75-Day Transition

The book of Daniel indicates a mysterious 75-day period between Christ's return and the beginning of the millennial kingdom (Daniel 12:11-12). Likely, this is when everything that needs to take place in order to establish the millennial kingdom will occur. This could include the cleanup from the destruction of the armies of the antichrist, the renovation of the earth, and the wedding supper of the Lamb (scholars vary on where they place this latter event).

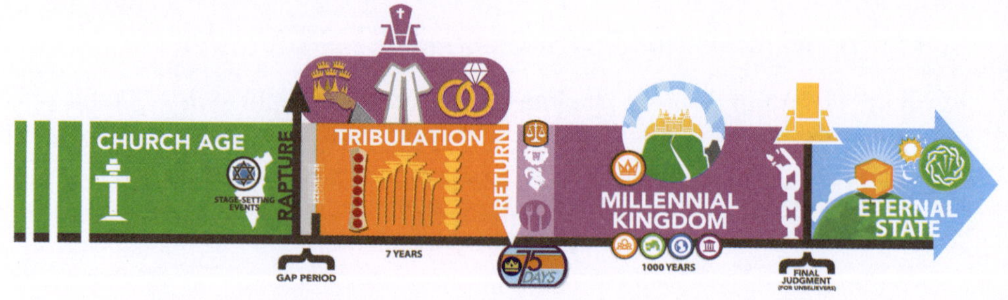

Getting the Full Picture

In case this is your first time studying the details of eschatology and how all these end-times pieces fit into the puzzle, I wanted to be sure to include all of this in a single chapter. Much like the logical and necessary chronology of a fighter's training camp, there is a logical and necessary chronology to all key end-times events. There are many more details and smaller puzzle pieces that we cannot be dogmatic about where they fit in or how they fall into place. But what I have presented in this chapter are the key puzzle pieces we can establish with a large amount of confidence.

As you continue studying these things, please do not simply take my word for it. Vet these details for yourself and as you do, you will find that your convictions about the order of events will become yours. More importantly, your relationship with the God of the Word will grow deeper and your appreciation for the Word of God will grow stronger.

With this macro view of the end times in mind, in the next chapter let us zoom in, slow down, and take a micro view of the main event we are waiting for as believers in Messiah.

SECTION 3:

THE BREAKDOWN

DIGGING INTO THE DETAILS

Slow Mo—A Frame-by-Frame Breakdown

Therefore, comfort one another with these words.

1 THESSALONIANS 4:18 (NASB)

It is likely you have heard of Wyatt Earp (1848–1929), the famous handlebar-mustache-sporting lawman of the American West. He was famous for being involved in many events, including the notable gunfight at the O.K. Corral in Tombstone, Arizona (1881), and the ensuing "cowboy war" that followed. Over the years, he has been depicted in various movies and television shows.

But it may surprise you to know that years after the tough and notable law enforcement activities of the famed gunfighter, the retired Wyatt Earp was tapped as a referee for a heavyweight prizefight that was held in San Francisco in 1896 between Bob Fitzsimmons and Tom Sharkey.[1]

During the fight, Fitzsimmons seemed to outmatch Sharkey in every round. The outcome seemed inevitable until Fitzsimmons threw a body shot that dropped Sharkey to the floor. Sharkey's corner immediately screamed foul and claimed the punch was a low blow. Whether it was clever acting on the part of Sharkey, or it was indeed a low blow, Earp suddenly declared Sharkey the winner by way of disqualification.

The crowd went crazy, as did Fitzsimmons's corner. The latter immediately claimed that the fight had been fixed. This incident stuck with Earp and is still debated and discussed by boxing fans to this day. Was it a fixed fight? Was the outcome the result of an inexperienced referee, an honest mistake, or a legitimate disqualification? We will never know. One reason being this event occurred only one year after projected moving pictures were invented,[2] and roughly 65 years before slow-motion replay began to be used in televised sports. The technology of slow-motion replay was first put into widespread use on November 25, 1961, during ABC's broadcast of a college football game between Boston College and Syracuse.[3]

Had there been video cameras and instant-replay capabilities available during the infamous fight refereed by Wyatt Earp, we could simply roll back the tape and step through time frame by frame to get some answers on what actually happened.

In his word, God provides a moment-by-moment order of events for the rapture. In this chapter, though we will not be viewing any film, we are going to look at a slow-motion breakdown of the details of the rapture. I will break down each key action as described in 1 Thessalonians 4:13-17. But first, let us consider the most detailed rapture passage of the Bible in its entirety so that it is fresh in our minds as we break it down frame by frame.

> We do not want you to be uninformed, brethren, about those who are asleep, so that you will not grieve as do the rest who have no hope. For if we believe that Jesus died and rose again, even so God will bring with Him those who have fallen asleep in Jesus. For this we say to you by the word of the Lord, that we who are alive and remain until the coming of the Lord, will not precede those who have fallen asleep. For the Lord Himself will descend from heaven with a shout, with the voice of the archangel and with the

> trumpet of God, and the dead in Christ will rise first. Then we who are alive and remain will be caught up together with them in the clouds to meet the Lord in the air, and so we shall always be with the Lord (NASB1995).

Considering the passage in its full context helps us to understand how each key action is connected. Before we look at the frame-by-frame details of the rapture (verses 16-17), I would like to establish the purpose of the apostle Paul's letter. Then, we will direct our attention to the preceding verses (verses 13-15) that help frame the context of this critically important revelation regarding the rapture of the church.

To provide some historical background, Paul planted the church at Thessalonica during his second missionary journey, along with Timothy and Silas. He was in Thessalonica for around three to four weeks before he was run off by unbelieving Jewish leaders in the area. In that short window of time, Paul and his team helped the new believers in Thessalonica establish a real and solid faith, grounding them in key theological truths and preparing them for the persecution they were likely to face.

In the book of 1 Thessalonians, Paul reminded the church of his personal example as he lived out the true faith in front of them. Then, he urged them to persevere through trials and struggles. He also comforted them regarding believers who have died (the context of this chapter). Of Paul's 13 letters, his two epistles to the Thessalonians include the most teaching he gave about the end times.

Eschatology was part of Paul's "New Believers 101" class, so to speak. The two epistles to the Thessalonians were among the first of Paul's letters to churches (AD 50–51), written soon after Paul's earliest letter that was written to the Galatians (AD 48). These letters closely followed the earliest written New Testament letter by James (AD 44–48). This shows us that very early in church history the chronological details of eschatology were part of the basic doctrine taught to believers.

With that small bit of background, let's pivot to the verses that help set up the actual description of the rapture of the church. First, notice in verse 13 that Paul is responding to the concerns that the Thessalonians had about the persecution they were facing and the deaths of some of their fellow believers. Regarding the prophetic layout of the future, Paul said that he did not want the Thessalonians to be uninformed about prophetic events. This flies in the face of modern church trends that bench or sideline Bible prophecy and eschatology because the topics are assumed to be unimportant and divisive.

In verse 14, the apostle ties the resurrection of Christ to the rapture of the church. Where the head goes, the body will go as well. The historical resurrection of

Christ guarantees our future resurrection. The rapture of the church is beautifully tied to the resurrection of our Savior. To put it another way: Easter leads to the rapture!

Also in verse 14, Paul mentions "those who have fallen asleep." This is—by its context and in the culture—a reference to believers who have died. In Scripture, sleep was commonly used as a euphemism for death (for example, see Genesis 47:30; Deuteronomy 31:16: 1 Kings 2:10; 22:40). Paul reminds the Thessalonian church that we do not grieve as the world grieves because we know that while the bodies of the dead in Christ are asleep, their spirits are with Christ who will bring them with him at the moment of the rapture (verse 14)!

Aren't you glad that the Lord is a God of restoration and that both our spirits and our bodies are of value? We are a complex makeup of spirit and body—made in the image of the Lord. Rather than discarding the bodies of believers, the Lord will resurrect and reunite them with the spirits of those who are dead in Christ. Right now, believers who are in heaven are there with the Lord in their spirit form, awaiting the moment they will receive their resurrected and glorified bodies. Even the dead in Christ still have amazing things to look forward to!

There are a few key things I would like to note from verse 15 as well. First, notice the key teaching about the rapture is not Paul's opinion or conjecture. It is "by the word of the Lord" (NASB1995). This is divine revelation from God. Those who downplay, ignore, or denigrate the teaching of the rapture, as John puts it in Revelation 22:19, take words away from the prophecies of the Bible. That, my friends, is dangerous ground.

Also notice that Paul thought the rapture was going to occur in his lifetime. He says "*we* who are alive and remain" (1 Thessalonians 4:17 NASB1995). This supports the doctrine of imminency (detailed in earlier chapters) and displays the attitude and expectation that all believers in the church age should have in every generation. The rapture is a signless event that could occur at any moment. In fact, there is not a single passage of Scripture that tells Christians to look for anything to happen prior to the rapture!

Finally, notice in verse 15 that those who have died will get to go first. Those of us who are alive will not precede them. Perhaps it is because they have been waiting longer. I sometimes joke that perhaps it is because they have six more feet to rise than we do. Perhaps it is so we who are alive can witness the resurrection of those who are asleep. Whatever the purposes, Paul notes that detail here, then again in the frame-by-frame breakdown of the details of the rapture.

With that bit of background and immediate context, let us turn our attention to the slow-motion, frame-by-frame details of the future rapture of the church.

Order of Events

The frame-by-frame details of the subevents of the rapture will likely happen in extremely quick succession—some perhaps simultaneously. Though we are not told explicitly if there is any amount of time between the details. It seems to me—from the details of the meaning of the word *harpazō*, along with the understanding that this future event will be an invasion into enemy territory—that the details of the rapture event will most likely occur in rapid succession.

First, the Lord himself will come down with a shout. Will he shout, "Come forth!" as he did when he raised Lazarus from the dead? (John 11:43 NASB1995). Will he shout, "Come up here!" like he did with John in Revelation 4? We can only speculate, but I believe Christians will hear his unmistakable shout as he suddenly cracks open our plane of existence somewhere in the sky—right in the heart of the enemy's territory.

Second, we will hear the voice of the archangel. This shout is likely a war cry given as the enemy's territory is invaded. It could also be the announcement of the Groom (Jesus) coming to gather the bride (the church) as was the custom in ancient Jewish wedding traditions. Or perhaps, it is both.

Perhaps this will be the archangel Michael, who leads God's armies and protects Israel against Satan's forces in Revelation 12. Michael is specifically referenced in the books of Daniel and Jude. In the book of Daniel, Michael is depicted as battling against regional fallen angels in order to get a critical prophetic message from God to Daniel.

Michael seems to be God's top general, perhaps the same rank that Satan had before he rebelled against God. In Jude 9, the definite article is used when referring to the archangel. This may indicate Michael is the only archangel. Yet, in Daniel 10:13, Michael is noted to be "one of the chief princes." So another possibility is that there are other archangels that are not named in Scripture.

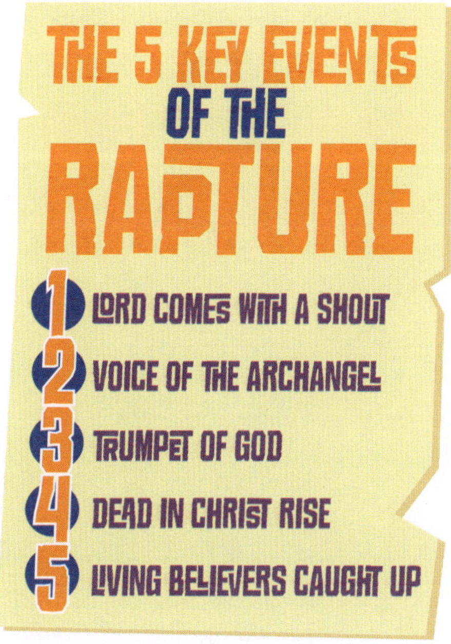

Perhaps the archangel of 1 Thessalonians 4 will be a different archangel tasked with the protection of the church and who will bring the announcement of this all-important event. It makes sense to me that God would have two distinct top-tier angels related to his two distinct programs—namely Israel and the church. We are left to speculate a bit and get to look forward to finding out exactly who this rapture archangel is when the rapture occurs.

Third, we will hear the trumpet of God—a distinctive blowing of a horn to call people to battle or to assembly for an important meeting or celebration. Both uses are applicable here.

Fourth, the dead in Christ will rise. This is the long-promised resurrection. What the Bible refers to as the first resurrection and the rapture are the same event. These church-age believers who have already died will receive their glorified bodies fit for heaven.

Fifth and finally, this passage tells us that we who are still alive will be caught up with the other church-age believers to meet the Lord in the air. Just as believers who are resurrected from the dead will receive bodies fit for heaven, we who are alive will also be instantly changed into new bodies. Can you imagine the joy as living believers are reunited with loved ones who have preceded them in death, and they are all standing together before the Lord Jesus Christ in all his glory?

What can be more exciting than this? One generation of Christians will not see death. Instead, they will be changed and snatched up to God's throne in a millisecond and will remain with the Lord forever. It is possible that we are that generation.

With that play-by-play, slow-motion overview of the key text related to the rapture fresh in your mind, I would like you to take a look at the other key rapture text in its fuller context. I have cited 1 Corinthians 15:52 as a key verse, but let's take a few moments to read the fuller context of verses 50-57. There we read:

> Now I say this, brothers and sisters, that flesh and blood cannot inherit the kingdom of God; nor does the perishable inherit the imperishable. Behold, I am telling you a mystery; we will not all sleep, but we will all be changed, in a moment, in the twinkling of an eye, at the last trumpet; for the trumpet will sound, and the dead will be raised imperishable, and we will be changed. For this perishable must put on the imperishable, and this mortal must put on immortality. But when this perishable puts on the imperishable, and this mortal puts on immortality, then will come about the saying that is written: "Death has been swallowed up in victory. Where, O Death, is your victory? Where, O Death, is your sting?" The sting of death is sin, and the power of sin is the Law; but thanks be to God, who gives us the victory through our Lord Jesus Christ (NASB).

Wow! Does that passage describing the resurrection/rapture not get you excited and make you appreciate all that God has done? There is so much to unpack there, but here are a few points that I do not want you to miss. First, our natural bodies are not fit for heaven. We would explode on impact. The resurrection to our glorified bodies is needed just before we are raptured so that we can handle the sights, sounds, and experiences of heaven. Flesh and blood—our natural bodies—cannot inherit the kingdom of God.

We will not all sleep. This phrase lines up with Paul's rapture passage in 1 Thessalonians 4:17, "We who are alive and remain" (NASB1995). Again, one generation of believers will not see death. We will be changed in the "twinkling of an eye." Recall, my friend Jeff Kinley points out to audiences that this is the Greek word *atomos*, which means: a period of time that cannot be divided. It will happen so quickly that the electrical impulses of the massive physical change will not even have time to travel to our fallen brains before our entire makeup is physically changed into our glorified state.

At that moment when the trumpet sounds, death will have no sting. Even now, the sting of death is only a threat because we know that this promised future moment is as good as done. It is only a matter of time.

What about you? What comes to mind when you think about the rapture? Instead of excitement and joy, many experience fear, apathy, or confusion. In Titus 2:13, Paul says we should be looking for the rapture and he calls it our "blessed hope." The problem is we have an enemy who wants to steal our hope and blur our understanding of this momentous event. The only way to fight his strategy is to look directly at the issue and carefully study what the Bible has to say about it.

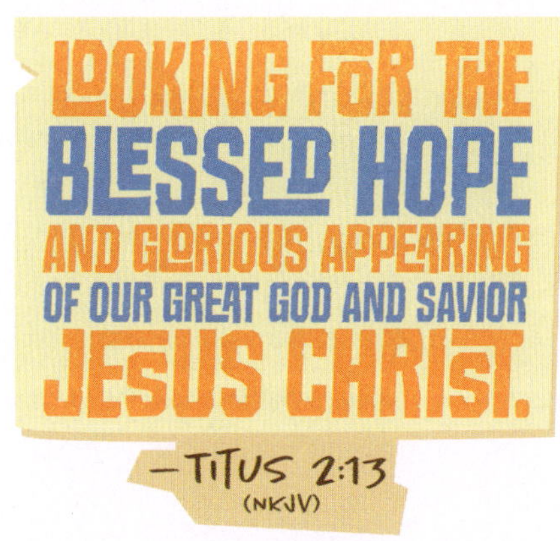

Frame-by-Frame Excitement

Isn't it amazing that the Lord has given us so many clear details about the rapture? It would be one thing if this prophesied future event was briefly mentioned, but God is not the author of confusion. He wanted us to know the frame-by-frame details of this momentous future event that we are destined for as believers in the Messiah! Like every good parent, our heavenly Father saw fit to make sure we had a clear grasp on the hope-filled doctrine of the rapture. What could be more exciting? To reiterate Paul's concluding application of this key rapture passage—1 Thessalonians 4—"Therefore comfort one another with these words"! (verse 18 NASB1995).

CHAPTER 11

The Removal of the Restrainer

The mystery of lawlessness is already at work; only He who now restrains will do so until He is removed. Then that lawless one will be revealed.

2 THESSALONIANS 2:7-8 (NASB)

Seasoned professional referee Mills Lane (1937–2022) is in the boxing hall of fame, not so much for boxing (though he did have a boxing career in the 1960s), but for officiating many famous matches.[1] The 150-pound, five-foot seven-inches, world-famous referee officiated several heavyweight championship matches from the 1970s through the 1990s—refereeing fighters who were up to 100 pounds heavier, a foot and a half taller, and 30 years younger than he was. Despite these notable differences, Mills Lane controlled the bouts with impeccable prowess, professionalism, and authority.

Any of the heavyweights could have knocked Mills Lane clear out of the ring, but the seasoned referee had one thing on his side—the full weight and authority of the boxing governing board. The unseen power of the governing authority embodied in a surprisingly frail (by comparison) entity (the small referee) kept massive fighters in line until the final bell.

Unique to the church age is the fact that the Holy Spirit indwells each believer. This was not the case in times past, but began on the day of Pentecost. The New Testament informs believers that we are the temple of the Holy Spirit. We are also referred to as the salt of the world and the light of the world. One of the main purposes of salt in the ancient world was to slow decay. The purpose of light is to shine in dark places to expose what is there and to help others see truth.

Though we church-age believers are frail, imperfect, and weak in and of ourselves, we are indwelled by the Holy Spirit who helps us restrain evil, delay the decay, and shine light into dark places. We do not fully realize just how much evil we are restraining simply by being here. That is one reason God calls believers to work on all areas of society, gives us spiritual gifts to edify the church, and calls each of us to a unique work that only we can perform.

In 2 Thessalonians 2, Paul makes mention of a restrainer—one who is holding back the global tide of evil and instability needed in order for the future antichrist to step onto the world scene. The restraining influence of the Spirit-indwelled church is the strongest force on the planet right now.

We read this in verses 6-8, "You know what restrains him now, so that he will be revealed in his time. For the mystery of lawlessness is already at work; only He who now restrains will do so until He is removed. Then that lawless one will be revealed, whom the Lord will eliminate with the breath of His mouth and bring to an end by the appearance of His coming" (NASB).

Context Is Key

If you'll recall, Paul wrote two letters to the Thessalonians. The occasion of the first letter was Paul's response to the report Timothy brought back to Paul (who was in Corinth, but sent Timothy to check on the young church). Some of the Thessalonians had stopped working, assuming the Lord's return was at hand.

Idle hands are not good, and this led some of the Thessalonians to fall back into their old ways. Some were also concerned about their loved ones who had died. So Paul wanted to address these (and other) issues. He implored them

to stay busy working while they wait for the Lord's return, and (as we have seen in the previous chapter) he addressed the issue of the believers who had recently died.

The main reason for Paul's second letter was to clear up some confusion (brought by some false teachers) regarding the timing of the future tribulation period—known as the Day of the Lord. Due to persecution the Thessalonian believers were facing, someone had convinced the Thessalonian believers that they had already entered the Day of the Lord (2:1-2), also known as the tribulation period. Paul assured them this was not the case, and said that the apostasy and the revealing of the antichrist had to occur first (verse 3). Paul also assured his readers that the antichrist could not be revealed until the restrainer was removed (verses 6-8).

This is a very important point. Today, many people play pin-the-tail-on-the-antichrist and attempt to paint various world leaders as a potential candidate. But the passage above reveals that nobody will know who this person is until after the restrainer is removed. So the question is: Who is the restrainer?

I believe the restrainer is the Holy Spirit-indwelled church, and that the antichrist's rise to power will be kept from occurring until after the rapture has taken place. On the flip side, God's active judgment (that is, the Day of the Lord) will also be restrained until Christ takes his bride (the church—see Ephesians 5:23) out of the way of judgment (1 Thessalonians 5:9; Revelation 3:10), as has been his pattern in all biblical accounts of God removing the righteous before his active wrath falls. Remember Noah and Lot.

Notice in 2 Thessalonians 2, the restrainer is referred to both as a *what* (verse 6) and a *he* (verse 7). The *what* is the church and the *he* is the Holy Spirit. Also notice that the Holy Spirit will not cease to be omnipresent, but his unique restraining influence through the church will be taken out of the way in order to let the end-times drama of the ages begin.

This makes complete sense considering the church age began with the arrival of the Holy Spirit on the day of Pentecost, who was sent to indwell believers (John 16:7; 1 John 4:4; Romans 8:9; 1 Corinthians 6:19). In the Old Testament, this was not the case. The Spirit would come and go as the Lord willed. With the help of the Holy Spirit, each church-age believer serves as salt and light (Matthew 5:13-16) designed to delay the decay and shine bright rays into dark places—exposing evil. At the end of this age, the church (along with the indwelling Holy Spirit) will be removed. *Then*, the antichrist can be revealed.

This lines up with other passages as well. For example, in Daniel 7, the antichrist is depicted as a "little horn" that arises out of obscurity and overtakes three other horns. Horns represent power and both Revelation and Daniel speak of ten end-times rulers who will arise, then after them, the antichrist will arise and overtake three of them.

The book of Daniel provides the most complete picture of the antichrist found in the Old Testament. I use this pop-culture term *antichrist* because it is familiar to most, although this term is not found in the book of Daniel, nor in the book of Revelation. This yet-future evil end-times ruler is referred to as the antichrist only in the books of 1 and 2 John. This individual is given several titles in Scripture, but *antichrist* seems to have become the term that encapsulates them all. There are more than 100 passages that refer to this evil end-times ruler.

DEAR CHILDREN, THIS IS THE LAST HOUR;
AND AS YOU HAVE HEARD THAT THE
ANTICHRIST IS COMING,
EVEN NOW MANY ANTICHRISTS HAVE COME.
THIS IS HOW WE KNOW IT IS THE LAST HOUR.

—1 JOHN 2:18

Daniel 7 refers to the antichrist as the little horn (verse 8) and gives us some details about his rise to power and some other characteristics. When Daniel asked to be told the meaning of the prophecy, he was given the following information about the antichrist:

> The ten horns are ten kings who will come from this kingdom. After them another king will arise, different from the earlier ones; he will subdue three kings. He will speak against the Most High and oppress his holy people and try to change the set times and the laws. The holy people will be delivered into his hands for a time, times and half a time (verses 24-25).

So from 2 Thessalonians 2 and Daniel 7 we can logically conclude that the antichrist will not arise until after the rapture and after ten rulers are in place governing some form of an end-times revived Roman Empire.

The Domino That Starts It All

Think about this for a moment: At the moment of the rapture, there will be no believers on earth for the first time since the fall of mankind in the garden of Eden. Even there, God immediately took the life of an animal as a sacrifice and covered the sin of Adam and Eve.

At the moment of the rapture, not a single righteous person will be left on the planet. The restraining influence of the Holy Spirit-indwelled church will be removed and evil will crash in on the world like never before. Evil will have no bounds. The ensuing chaos after the rapture will be the perfect scenario for the charismatic and influential antichrist to step onto the scene.

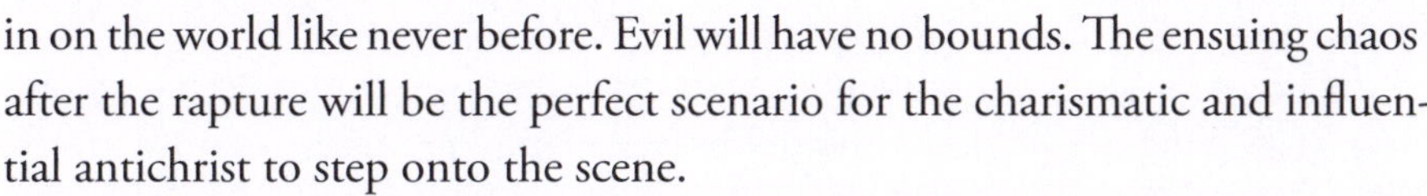

But there is some good news for even those left behind. Fairly quickly, many postrapture people will become believers through the witness of the two witnesses, the 144,000, and the combined resources and lingering testimonies left behind by church-age believers. The greatest revival in history will take place after the rapture.

But these saints will not be part of the church. They will be in a new era when evil rules the world, a covenant will be confirmed, and 21 judgments directly from the hand of God will be unleashed on the earth in a short seven-year period. Unfortunately, it will also be a time when the world will persecute and kill believers like never before.

Very early in the judgments, we find that the fifth seal judgment is that of martyrdom (Revelation 6:9-11). After the sixth seal judgment, we bump into an interlude in Revelation 7. There we discover the ministry of the 144,000. After their introduction, the next thing we read about is "a great multitude that no one could count" from every corner of the earth standing before the throne and the Savior (verse 9).

Recounting the Restrainer

Revisionist history and cancel culture aside, one can't honestly overlook the positive and game-changing impact that true biblical Christianity has had on the world. History cannot be told without it. Democracies and free nations would not exist without it. Christianity has played a major role in religious freedom, the abolishing of slavery, the key discoveries of science, the founding of great nations, the collapse of evil nations, technology and innovation, the arts, and so much more.

Today's secularists increasingly portray the effects of Christianity on the world as negative. Indeed, many evils have been done in the name of religion, but in every case, they were contrary to true biblical Christianity. Wherever true biblical Christianity has gone, it has been a change agent for good. The fact is biblical Christianity, when applied, serves to bring unity and order, make nations more prosperous, elevate the position of the poor and mistreated, break down racial barriers, bring peace, expose corruption, and counter the evils of the day—including slavery, human trafficking, and abortion.

Christianity has had such a global impact that history literally cannot be told without acknowledging this fact. History itself is divided by the life of Christ. When it comes to calendar years, while modern academia uses terms such as CE (common era) and BCE (before the common era), these terms are just a veiled attempt to remove the influence of Christ from history. For centuries, history has been cataloged as taking place either before Christ (BC) or *anno domini* (AD), which is Latin for "in the year of the Lord."

As history marched forward, Christianity's spread and impact on the Roman Empire transitioned into its impact on Europe and the entire West via the various colonies that came out of Europe—including America. At the same time, it took root in various pockets in Africa and the Middle East. Later, during the great missionary movement of the nineteenth century, the gospel was taken to the Far East.

With the advent of modern technologies such as satellite TV and shortwave radio, the gospel has literally gone out all over the world and continues to do so today through the internet and other means. Even the countries that are the most closed off to Christianity—such as North Korea, Iran, China, and multiple Islamic nations in Africa and Asia—are hearing the gospel through modern technology.

Scripture teaches that the church (all true believers everywhere) is the salt and light of the world. As evil as this world is, it would surely have already imploded without the preserving influence of salt and the truth-exposing light of the church. We will not fully appreciate the impact the Bible has had on the world until we are in heaven.

Whole books have been written on each sphere of influence that has been directly impacted by the truths of Scripture and the influence of Bible-believing

Christians—including education, hospitals, serving the poor, the family unit, justice, language, diplomacy, science, technology, work, sound business practices, and so much more.

There is not an area of life that the Bible does not address. It is the owner's manual for all things human. The principles found in the Bible truly work. Scripture is God-breathed. It is the written inspired Word of God, full of wisdom and given as a gift to the world. To the extent we apply it, we are blessed by it.

As a change agent, the Bible disrupts evil systems. Satan does not like to give up territory, but in every single case, Truth with a capital *T* will win the day. As you and I study the Bible and put it into practice, we will face resistance, but we must boldly and lovingly proclaim truth to a world that desperately needs it. We are called to be the salt of the earth and the light of the world (Matthew 5:13-16) as long as we are able to do so. The future removal of the Restrainer is one and the same as the rapture of the church. All salt will be removed. All light shut off. Then the world will be readied for the final act of the ages.

CHAPTER 12

Past, Present, and Future Aspects of Salvation

I am confident of this very thing, that He who began a good work among you will complete it by the day of Christ Jesus.

PHILIPPIANS 1:6 (NASB)

Cus D'Amato knew Mike Tyson would be a champion the moment he first trained him as a youngster. Coach D'Amato was an old-school boxer with an extremely high ring and training IQ. Having previously trained International Boxing Hall of Famers Floyd Patterson and José Torres, Cus D'Amato knew when his gut was right.

As an avid boxing historian, D'Amato tapped into some of the forgotten aspects of the sweet science that would prove to be the perfect fit for young Tyson. Techniques such as the peek-a-boo defense, the aggressive bob-and-weave offense that got Tyson into close range to land power shots on his much larger opponents, and maximizing the use of Tyson's low center of gravity to drop out of the punching range of his longer-armed opponents. These and other tactics proved to be what D'Amato knew would produce one of the greatest fighters of all time.

Coach D'Amato tapped into the history of the past to custom craft a style that matched Tyson's build and natural abilities. The legendary coach said he knew as soon as he saw Tyson train that the fighter would become a champion. Cus focused on patiently training the young fighter in the present and was convinced that their carefully chosen path would make Tyson one of the most legendary heavyweight champions of all time.

Mike Tyson became the youngest heavyweight champion of the world on November 22, 1986, at age 20 (and four months),[1] breaking the previous record held by Floyd Patterson (21 years and 10 months).[2] Boxing Hall of Famer Patterson held the record for almost 30 years (only eight days shy to be exact).[3] Less than a year later, on August 1, 1987, Tyson became the first undisputed heavyweight champion in the complicated era of three governing bodies by winning the remaining of the three belts in a bout against Tony Tucker.

Sadly, when his mentor and father figure Cus died, Tyson's tough childhood and some bad choices caused him to spiral downward. His personal life was a tragedy, and his choices landed him in prison for three years and in various levels of bankruptcy until after his retirement from boxing.

But I bring up this historical account of a legendary coach who tapped into the past, crafted a plan in the present, with full conviction of what would come to pass in the future to highlight a central aspect of the doctrine of the rapture that is easy to overlook.

Three Aspects of Salvation

Past

Often when we talk about salvation, we focus on the work of the cross and the resurrection—and understandably so. The passion week was the apex of world history. God became flesh, lived a perfect life, died on a brutal Roman cross for our sins, and was raised from the dead on the third day securing complete victory over sin and death.

His righteousness is credited to our account. This is the scandal of grace, that Jesus trades our sin for his perfection. Scripture puts it this way, "He made Him who knew no sin to be sin in our behalf, so that we might become the righteousness of God in Him" (2 Corinthians 5:21 NASB).

Those critical first-century events of the death, burial, and resurrection of the Messiah form the epicenter of our faith and practice as Christians. We are a people of reflection as we look back to those events. Belief in those events and our trust in the long-awaited Messiah for the forgiveness of sins is what saves us. If you have trusted Christ as your Savior, you are saved.

Note that term. *Saved.* It is past tense. It is accomplished. Or as Jesus himself said it on the cross, "It is finished" (John 19:30). But there is so much more! There are actually three aspects to our salvation—a past, present, and future aspect.

Present

While we are incredibly blessed to have the Holy Spirit indwelling us as believers in the church age, we are reminded daily that we still have a sin nature. We are born with a fallen nature that gravitates away from God and toward destructive things instead. After the rebellion of Adam and Eve, humans were born with this sin nature and we choose sin ourselves. Our sinfulness stands in extreme contrast with the holiness of God. The sinfulness of mankind has us under a curse, under the wrath of God, and causes us to be completely spiritually dead—in need of a miraculous rescue.

Once a person becomes a believer in Christ they are seen as righteous by God. Our sinfulness was placed on Christ at the cross. He was our substitute. He took our punishment. But practically speaking, believers now live with a tension between our fallen nature and our new life of faith. Paul calls it "the flesh" (Romans 7:5).

Before Christ we were slaves to the flesh. We had no choice but to follow its dictates. But when someone is saved—when they believe in Jesus and decide to follow him—the Holy Spirit (one of the members of the three-in-one God) comes to reside in each believer. Simply put, God (the Holy Spirit) never leaves a Christian once they accept Christ.

Since the Holy Spirit dwells with the believer who still has their old nature (the flesh), there is an ongoing tension between the two. But now, the difference is the believer no longer needs to follow the flesh. They have a choice. The same Spirit who raised Jesus from the dead now indwells, regenerates, and empowers the believer to overcome the pull of the flesh.

But the flesh has other challenges to be addressed as well. After the fall and before Christ, the law was given. But Paul highlights the fact that the law merely makes people want to sin more. Once they know what is off-limits, the flesh desires those things all the more. But grace works differently. Grace lifts us up out of an impossible situation that the law was powerless to do. Grace brings spiritually dead people to life. But there is another challenge that arises—legalism. After one is saved by grace through faith at a certain point in time (when they choose to follow Christ), they may be tempted to live life by their own power. Spiritual disciplines can easily become checkboxes that make one righteous in their own eyes. The Spirit-led believer must be consciously aware of the drift toward legalism and walk by faith daily.

Is it any wonder that the apostle Paul—a genuine spiritual giant and writer of most of the New Testament letters—wrote this in Romans 7:15-21:

> I do not understand what I do. For what I want to do I do not do, but what I hate I do. And if I do what I do not want to do, I agree that the law is good. As it is, it is no longer I myself who do it, but it is sin living in me. For I know that good itself does not dwell in me, that is, in my sinful nature. For I have the desire to do what is good, but I cannot carry it out. For I do not do the good I want to do, but the evil I do not want to do—this I keep on doing. Now if I do what I do not want to do, it is no longer I who do it, but it is sin living in me that does it. So I find this law at work: Although I want to do good, evil is right there with me.

Thankfully, after the conclusion of chapter 7, Paul includes this verse in Romans 8:1, "Therefore there is now no condemnation at all for those who are in Christ Jesus" (NASB).

So while we needed a Savior to secure our salvation in the past, we still need a Savior to save us from our own sin nature in the present. Thank God for grace. Thank God for forgiveness. Thank God for patience. Thank God that our salvation is not based on our works, but on his perfect righteousness that changes us day by day to become more like the Savior and saves us in the present!

Future

Finally, there is a key future aspect to our salvation—the moment of the rapture! Continuing our excerpts from Paul's magnum opus and theological treatise on the core features of God's plan of salvation, we read this mind-bending and mysterious proclamation in Romans 8:29-30: "Those whom He foreknew, He also predestined to become conformed to the image of His Son, so that He would be the firstborn among many brothers and sisters; and these whom He predestined, He also called; and these whom He called, He also justified; and these whom He justified, He also glorified" (NASB).

Note the past aspect of our salvation that reaches to eternity past (those he foreknew), the present aspect of God's active work in our lives (justifying us and conforming us to the image of his Son), and the future aspect of our salvation (whom he justified, he also glorified).

Also note that from God's eternal perspective, all three aspects are viewed in the past tense. God—the Creator of time and Sovereign of history—sees our glorification as already taken place. It is as good as done.

From our perspective, we have not yet been glorified. We are stuck in chronological time. God is not. To us, our glorification is yet future and will occur at the moment of the rapture. One day soon—when Jesus again steps out of heaven and into the clouds with a shout and a trumpet blast—the dead in Christ will rise in glorified form, and then we who are still alive will be instantly transformed and receive our glorified bodies!

How Then Should We Live?

Just to recap, the three aspects of our salvation are as follows. As believers in Christ, we *have been saved* from the penalty of sin (regeneration/justification); we *are being saved* from the power of sin as we grow to be more like Christ in our discipleship (sanctification); and one day we *will be saved* from the very presence of sin in our body and in the world (glorification).

The rapture will be the moment that our full promised salvation will be complete! Redemption is the first phase of our salvation. Restoration is salvation completed. God created our bodies and looks forward to our full and complete restoration. God never discards what he creates; he redeems and restores it.

We must leave people with the hope that comes from an understanding that a day is coming when God will set everything straight and our salvation will be complete. As we point people back to the cross to celebrate redemption, we must also point them upward to remind them that God is still on the throne (and guiding their lives currently), and we must point them to our promised future when God will fulfill every prophetic promise, reward his own, and restore all things.

We are to be a people of reflection and anticipation. As we reflect on what has been accomplished on the cross and through the resurrection, we walk by faith in the present with the understanding that God is growing us toward Christlikeness, and we anticipate our complete physical and spiritual salvation that will occur at the moment of the rapture—in the twinkling of an eye. Dear believer, live in great anticipation of this coming moment and let it guide your actions, emotions, and choices today!

SECTION 4:

THE BOTTOM LINE

THE CHAMPIONSHIP FIGHT IS ON!
IT'S ONLY A MATTER OF TIME

Times of the Signs—A Look at the Current Convergence

Not giving up meeting together, as some are in the habit of doing, but encouraging one another—and all the more as you see the Day approaching.

HEBREWS 10:25

One of the most revered arenas for boxing is New York City's Madison Square Garden. Housed above Penn Station in Manhattan, the venue was named after the fourth president of the United States and has been host to a wide variety of events, most notably those featuring major boxing prizefights.

The complex's current iteration is the fourth structure in the history of the venue, with the first three being constructed in 1873, 1879—when it was first named Madison Square Garden (torn down in 1890)—and 1925. The current building was constructed in 1968.[1]

Since its second iteration (1879) and forward, the venue has been home to a plethora of famous and notable boxing events, including the 1927 Golden Gloves tournament. It has also hosted historical heavyweight bouts, including Rocky Marciano versus Joe Louis in 1951, Muhammad Ali versus Joe Frazier in 1971, and Lennox Lewis versus Evander Holyfield in 1999, just to name a few.[2]

The arena has a fight-day crowd capacity of 20,789 and is affectionately referred to as simply "The Garden." The original boxing ring used in MSG II and MSG III was moved to the Boxing Hall of Fame in 2007, after 82 years of service.[3]

Other defining events at The Garden include the first NBA championship of the New York Knicks (1970, and again in 1973), John Lennon's final performance (1974), and the New York Rangers' Stanley Cup Finals victory (1994).[4]

With headliner boxing events occurring at night, the undercard usually begins around 7:00 p.m., with the main event usually scheduled for midnight—although this main event start time can be shuffled forward if one or more of the earlier bouts ends early due to a knockout (KO), technical knockout (TKO), or disqualification.

You can imagine the large amount of preparation for such an event and the number of things that must occur before the gates open and the first patron is allowed into the arena that evening. Floors must be swept. Food courts stocked. Security measures enabled. Ring assembled. Floor seats set up. Lights checked. Cameras and technology tested.

Aside from the arena's preparation, the various participants must be readied. Obviously, the boxers must have the day's schedule meticulously planned. So too, all the support staff for the event, arena, and secondary support. New York City police officers are briefed and readied. Judges and ringside announcers prepare for the evening's activities. Last, but not least, each ticket holder plans their day so they can be ready in time to travel to the arena and find their seat before the matches begin.

To abbreviate this necessary preparation, in the hours leading up to a major boxing event, The Garden will be transformed from a dark and empty echo chamber to a fully lit arena jam-packed with more than 20,000 people, complete with television cameras, press representatives, judges, high-decibel noise, and all of the logistical provisions to support that many people for four to six hours of boxing entertainment. If you have ever seen time-lapsed video footage of such a spectacle taking shape, you have witnessed in short order how various developments unfold that make an arena morph from an empty space to a venue teeming with activity, action, and excitement.

Well, as you and I look around it is clear to see that the stadium is filling up, the lights are beginning to dim, and the key participants are moving into place. The tribulation period is casting its shadow ahead of itself. In this generation, we are witnessing the arena being readied for earth's final events, which means that the rapture of the church is that much closer in proximity! With that in mind, I would like us to look at five key indicators that help demonstrate how the metaphorical arena is quickly filling up.

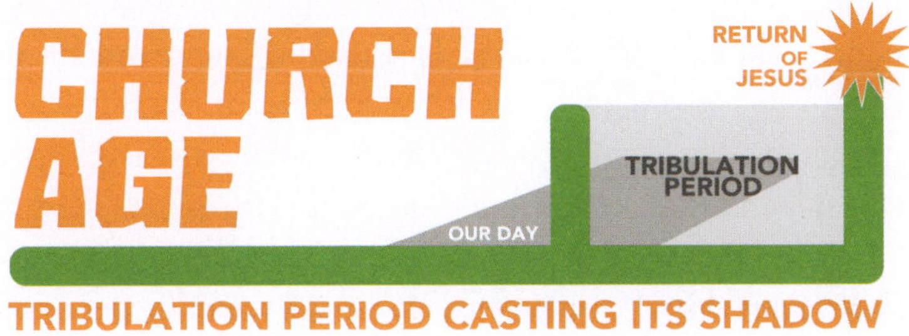

But first, I would like to address a question to assure you we are on solid biblical ground here. The question I would like to pose—because I have heard some Christians ask it as well—is this: Should we spend time and energy looking for indications that the Lord's return is near? In other words, are we expected to discern the times, or is that just an unhealthy distraction?

Should We Attempt to Discern the Times?

We are told in 1 Chronicles 12:32 that the leaders of Issachar "understood the signs of the times and knew the best course for Israel to take" (NLT). The wise men from the East (Matthew 2), the godly old man Simeon (Luke 2), and the old prophetess Anna (Luke 2) all understood the time frame of the Lord's first arrival, and their amazing stories are recorded for us in Scripture.

We also find that Jesus rebuked the Pharisees and the crowds of people for not knowing the signs of their day. To the scribes and Pharisees, he said, "You know how to interpret the weather signs in the sky, but you don't know how to interpret the signs of the times!" (Matthew 16:3 NLT). To the crowds he said, "You fools! You know how to interpret the weather signs of the earth and sky, but you don't know how to interpret the present times" (Luke 12:56 NLT).

In what is known as the Olivet Discourse, Jesus responded to a question asked by his disciples. After he had informed them that the beautiful temple and surrounding buildings they were admiring would be completely destroyed, Jesus' disciples approached him wanting to understand more. In Matthew 24:3, we read, "As Jesus was sitting on the Mount of Olives, the disciples came to him privately. 'Tell us,' they said, 'when will this happen, and what will be the sign of your coming and of the end of the age?'"

Rather than rebuke them or downplay the question, Jesus gave them a lengthy description of the key events of the future tribulation period. This central teaching by Jesus (his second-longest recorded sermon) regarding the end times is recorded in three of the four Gospels—Matthew 24, Mark 13, and Luke 21—and mirrors the chronology of many key details given to us in Revelation 6–19. Jesus clearly intended for his disciples (and those of us reading the inspired Word of God) to understand these details in order to discern their stage-setting development.

The Old Testament prophets and even the angels have longed to understand the time frame we are currently in. In 1 Peter 1:10-12, we read,

> Concerning this salvation, the prophets, who spoke of the grace that was to come to you, searched intently and with the greatest care, trying to find out the time and circumstances to which the Spirit of Christ in them was pointing when he predicted *the sufferings of the Messiah* [first coming] and *the glories that would follow* [second coming/millennial kingdom]. It was revealed to them that they were not serving themselves but you, when they spoke of the things that have now been told you by those who have preached the gospel to you by the Holy Spirit sent from heaven. Even angels long to look into these things (emphasis added, bracketed text for clarity).

Notice the key details I highlighted in the verses above. The prophets longed to understand the "time and circumstances" related to the first and second comings. In the midst of the struggle to live in our day we need to remember how blessed we are to see these things! Thankfully, God's people will be removed (via the rapture) prior to God's judgment of the world (as has been the clear pattern of his activity in times past and his stated intentions at the end of the age), but that doesn't mean we won't live in dangerous times prior to the rapture. In fact, 2 Timothy 3:1-5 tells us as much. We are not left uninformed.

The apostle Paul, whom God used to take Christianity to the Gentiles, realized that the church age was the last "age" or era before the rapture and the terrible tribulation period. He tells us in Romans 13:11-12, "This is all the more urgent, for you know how late it is; time is running out. Wake up, for our salvation is nearer now than when we first

believed. The night is almost gone; the day of salvation will soon be here" (NLT). If this was true in Paul's day, it's even truer today, because almost 2,000 years have passed. Paul also admonished believers to be watchful and ready.

Finally, the book of Hebrews provides the insight that those living close to Jesus' return will be able to recognize that the day of the Lord's return to set up the kingdom is approaching—meaning the rapture, which will occur at least seven years prior to the Messiah's return to earth is that much nearer on the horizon. Consider the bold statement in the latter part of Hebrews 10, where the writer sees Christians as "not giving up meeting together, as some are in the habit of doing, but encouraging one another—and all the more as you see the Day approaching" (verse 25).

Also note the admonition to encourage one another. Be reminded of Paul's words after describing the details of the rapture; he wrote, "Therefore encourage one another with these words" (1 Thessalonians 4:18). Clearly, believers at the end of the church age will be able to discern when the Day of the Lord is near. A careful study of Scripture demonstrates the fact that believers are instructed to watch for the Lord's return and understand their times.

Five Key End-Times Indicators

So with confidence in knowing Christians are called to discern the times, here are five key prophetic developments that indicate we are nearing the time of the end. It was tough to distill it down to only five, but here are what I consider the most compelling conditions for us to pay attention to as they continue to develop in our day.

Keep in mind these are (for the most part) stage-setting developments as opposed to the actual fulfillment of prophecy. For most of the prophecies detailed below (other than Israel's rebirth as a nation in unbelief), they are either in formation (like the Jewish people coming back to their ancient homeland) or are setting the stage for the future events of the tribulation period. Just to reiterate, prophecy does not occur in a vacuum. The stage must be set. We are clearly witnessing such preparations in our day—as no other generation has since the first century.

All Eyes on Israel

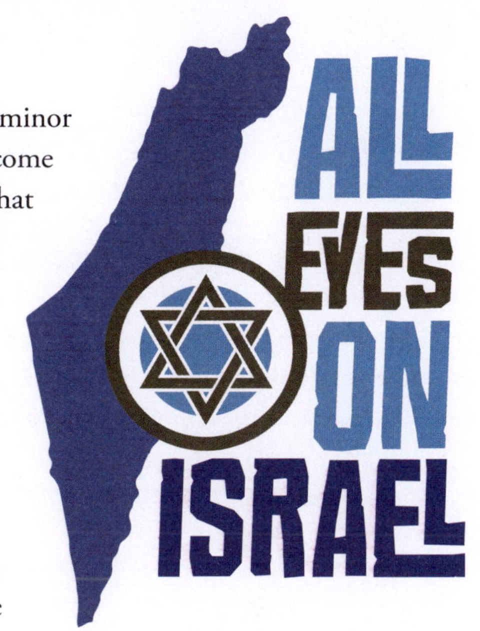

All the major prophets and most of the minor prophets predicted that Israel would become a nation again in the latter days, and that the focus of the world would be on this tiny nation. For some of these prophecies the context is the future tribulation period, for others the time frame in view is the future kingdom age. In either case, Israel's existence, being in control of Jerusalem, and having access to the temple mount are prerequisites for all key end-times events beginning with the confirming of a covenant by the future antichrist between Israel and many other nations.

In the New Testament, Jesus (in Matthew 24) and John (in Revelation 11–13, 16, and 19) also predict Israel will be a nation again, will be in full control of Jerusalem, and will control the temple mount prior to the midpoint of the future tribulation period.

Zechariah 12:3 and Revelation 16:14-16 predict that by the end of the tribulation period, the entire world will turn its back on Israel and gather to fight against God. The general thrust of the prophets, when speaking about Israel in the last days, is that the entire world will be fixated on this tiny piece of real estate, which is roughly the size of New Jersey and could fit into Lake Michigan with room to spare.

To summarize the stage-setting conditions and attitude of the world regarding Israel's clearly prophesied predicament in the future tribulation period, here is what we should expect to see as we are nearing those events. First, Israel will become a nation again after a long period of time of the Jewish people being scattered all over the world and terribly mistreated (Deuteronomy 28; Ezekiel 36–37). Check. This necessary phase of the prophecy was fulfilled in 1948. There are even hints to the fact that Israel would first be a nation primarily in unbelief, then at some point would receive God's Spirit (Ezekiel 37:6-14). This aligns with other prophecies related to the Jewish people finally calling on the Lord after being back in the land (Zechariah 12:10-14; Matthew 23:37-39; Romans 11:26).

Next, we should expect to see the Jewish people continually streaming back to their ancient homeland, the land and the cities springing back to life, and the surrounding countries attacking Israel with the stated purpose of destroying the tiny nation. This prophecy is in the process of being fulfilled right before our eyes. Some prophecies are prophetic conditions rather than specific events. The prophecies related to Israel will find complete fulfillment in the future kingdom age.

The closer we get to the tribulation period, the more we should expect to see Israel standing alone, being attacked by various players in the Middle East (and eventually Russia as well; see below), having a thriving economy and valuable natural resources, and desiring broad concrete agreements with her neighbors so she can finally dwell in peace. Now ask yourself this question: Do we see these conditions today? Have these conditions continued to increase in recent years? If you track Israel's modern statehood from 1948 to today, it is easy to see that she has faced these conditions with increasing frequency and intensity.

The Global Rise of Antisemitism

Along with several conditions related specifically to the reformed State of Israel, we should also expect to see a global rise in antisemitism. While this

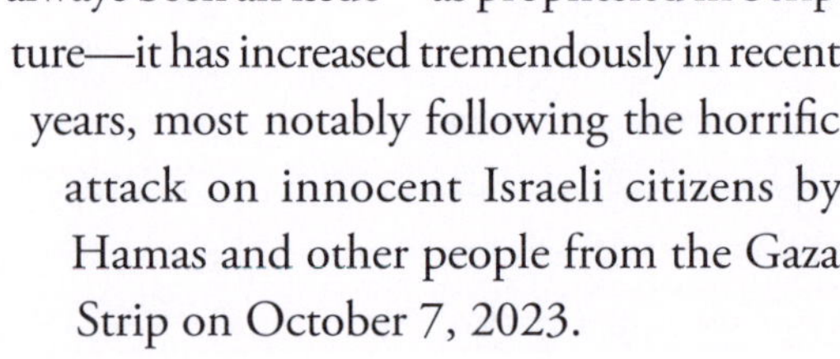

has always been an issue—as prophesied in Scripture—it has increased tremendously in recent years, most notably following the horrific attack on innocent Israeli citizens by Hamas and other people from the Gaza Strip on October 7, 2023.

Rather than showing sympathy to the people of Israel, within only a few days there were pro-Palestinian, Hamas-sympathizers rising up on college campuses and in various cities around the world calling for the destruction of Israel and the Jewish people. Jewish students and teachers had to stay away from their own college campuses while pro-Hamas demonstrators threatened and harassed them.

Even more telling is the fact that the global entity known as the United Nations consistently and overwhelmingly stands against Israel in their rhetoric and in their official resolutions. The prophetic symbolism cannot be missed. Through the United Nations, the entire world (with the exception of a few influential nations including the United States) repeatedly stands against the nation of Israel. I suspect that by the publishing of this book, antisemitism will have continued and increased. Now more than ever Christians need to stand with, protect, and encourage the Jewish people.

This is a stage-setting cultural phenomenon and is preparing the way for the events of the tribulation period. From the confirming of a covenant by a deceiver who will come on the scene appearing as a man of peace (Daniel 9; Revelation 6), to the tribulation-era holocaust of the Jewish people in the second half of the tribulation period (Revelation 12) where only one-third will survive (Zechariah 13:8)—modern day antisemitism is (as a good friend of mine calls it) end-times antisemitism.[5]

Satan hates the Jewish people and wants to annihilate them because of God's unconditional promises to them and because through the Jewish people God brought the Scriptures and the Savior to the world. Pertaining to the last days, Scripture predicts that at the end of the tribulation period the Jewish people will have their "blindness in part" (Romans 11:25 NKJV) removed and will finally call on their Messiah. This key future event is what will usher in the return of the Lord to save his people and destroy the enemy (Isaiah 63:1; Zechariah 12:10; Matthew 23:39; Romans 11:26; Revelation 12:6).

Satan knows prophecy and he is so self-deluded that he thinks he can thwart God's foreordained plans by destroying the Jewish people in the last days. If there are no Jewish people, there will be none to call upon the name of the Lord. This is at the heart of the current rise of antisemitism.

The current exponential increase in antisemitism is satanically energized and demonically activated. The enemy cannot wait to begin his plan. He is showing his cards. His hatred is out in the open. Sadly, we should expect to see this increase between now and the rapture.

Ezekiel 38 Alliance

Ezekiel 38 and 39 contain the most detailed account of any end-times war. These two chapters (which follow chronologically the prophecy of Israel's dry bones coming to life in Ezekiel 36–37) detail an end-times battle that will take place after the people of Israel are back in their homeland having been scattered and mistreated all over the world for a long period of time. Check. That part of the prophecy is fulfilled. After returning to their homeland and recovering from war, a group of nations that do not border Israel—led by Russia, Iran, and Turkey—attack Israel, specifically from her north but Syria will not be one of them.

All the nations (listed by their ancient names) are Islamic nations who are currently attempting to (or openly desiring to) attack Israel—except for Russia, who will be there leading the pack to take something valuable from Israel (oil, gas, natural resources, technology, etc.), and some of the other nations of the former Soviet bloc. Russia will serve as a guard for the others, but the main partnership will be between Russia, Iran, and Turkey. This partnership is currently in place and Syria is merely a puppet state being run by those three nations.

EZEKIEL 38 NATIONS

AND THEIR MODERN-DAY EQUIVALENTS

ANCIENT NAME	MODERN NAME
MAGOG	RUSSIA, CENTRAL ASIA
ROSH	RUSSIA
MESHECH	RUSSIA
TUBAL	RUSSIA OR TURKEY
PERSIA	IRAN
CUSH	ETHIOPIA, SUDAN
LUD	LIBYA, ALGERIA
GOMER	TURKEY
TOGARMAH	TURKEY, CENTRAL ASIA

On the opposite side of the equation, no other nation will come to Israel's rescue (God will, and he will show up in a major way). Saudi Arabia, the gulf states, and other nations will merely protest the invasion but will not come to Israel's aid in any meaningful way. The United States—Israel's main supporter since her founding in 1948—will either have removed its support or will be unable to respond militarily.

The stage for this end-times confrontation is nearly fully set and continues solidifying with each passing day. Note that this is a relatively recent development, having only really come together this century—yet it was predicted in detail 2,600 years ago! Keep an eye on this prophecy and the geopolitical developments related to it.

The Continued March of Globalism

When most people hear the term *globalism*, they usually think of the modern interconnectivity of global trade, commerce, travel, and culture. But what I'm referring to here is the widespread, specific, and intentional efforts of the world's most powerful influencers (international bankers, political leaders, and global-scale business leaders) to bring about a one-world government.

If you take the time to dig into the founding documents, websites, articles, and interviews of people in (and/or connected to) these organizations and initiatives, you will see that it is an established fact that they are trying (more now than ever) to bring about a one-world global government. It is important to note that this is not a left versus right issue. Prominent people from both sides of the proverbial aisle are globalists. Following are a handful of the well-funded, extremely influential organizations that are currently leveraging everything they can to form a real one-world government:

- The World Economic Forum
- The Great Reset
- The United Nations
- The 2030 Agenda
- The Council on Foreign Relations
- The Trilateral Commission
- The Council of the Americas
- The Americas Society
- The International Economic Forum of the Americas
- The Peterson Institute for International Economics

This is only the tip of the iceberg. Those are what you might call open globalist groups and initiatives. There are many smaller entities that coordinate to assist the organizations and initiatives listed above. So what does this have to do with eschatology? Well, the Bible teaches that after the rapture the ensuing chaos will quickly lead to a one-world government (see Daniel 2; 7; Revelation 13; 17) that will install a single leader whom we commonly refer to as the antichrist. Don't let the familiarity of those terms and passages breed contempt or form caricatured notions in your mind. Look around you as you research the various globalist initiatives.

In order for a one-world government to almost immediately form after the rapture, it is necessary that the plans and framework for such a thing must already be in place. And they are—along with all the technology necessary to pull it off. These facts are out in the open for all who are willing to take a look. This explains why great lengths are currently being taken to weaken America's national sovereignty. Our country is quickly becoming a shell of its former self. This fact is sad but true—and it lines up with Scripture as you will see further below. Thankfully, our true citizenship is in heaven. We can draw comfort from that even as our hearts break as we watch our once strong country weaken at an unprecedented rate.

The Need for Peace in the Middle East

Following the events of October 7, 2023, and the ensuing war dominos including all of Iran's proxies and Iran itself, there has never been a greater need for someone to establish peace in the Middle East. Every US president since Nixon has attempted to broker peace between Israel and her neighbors. At various times and in a variety of levels, Israel has had to defend herself from satanically led attacks on the tiny nation from the moment of her independence to today. Israel is tired. Her leaders are tired. Her citizens are tired.

It should be clear to her enemies by now that Israel is supernaturally protected and is not going anywhere. In Amos 9:15, God has informed us that "I will plant Israel in their own land, never again to be uprooted from the land I have given them." Yet the enemy thinks he can break prophecy and God's sovereign decrees.

The post-rapture chaos will provide the perfect environment, and Satan will provide the perfectly evil, smooth-talking broker of faux peace who will finally complete what many others have attempted—a peace agreement between Israel and her neighbors. The language of Daniel 9:27 suggests the antichrist will strengthen, complete, or possibly even force a peace treaty to be confirmed. Is it any coincidence that ever since Israel's founding in 1948, there has been a near-constant need for peace, and every US president since the early 1970s has been compelled to make an attempt at brokering peace in the region?

As we move closer to the timing of the rapture, keep an eye on this area of prophetic development and expect it to ramp up even more.

Convergence of Convergences

The fact that these conditions and many more that we could cite are converging in our day should get our attention. There are so many other categories and details we could discuss here, from the plans for a third temple in Israel, to technological developments, to the falling away of the church, to deception and corruption, to the rise of the occult and the open celebration of the demonic, to delusional thinking about God-ordained norms such as gender and marriage, and so much more.

CONVERGENCE

The rapid pace of these developments cannot be missed by anyone who is paying attention. While these developments are not good in themselves, they let us know that our exit draws near. All these conditions pertain to the future tribulation period, and as we have firmly established, the rapture of the church will occur prior to the beginning of that horrific prophesied period.

So while the enemy does his level best to discourage believers, we should flip the emotional script and view these events through the lens of God's prophetic Word so that we can live with joy, peace, and great anticipation of all that is in our promised future. The stadium is being readied for the main event!

Get Ready!

There is in store for me the crown of righteousness, which the Lord, the righteous Judge, will award to me on that day—and not only to me, but also to all who have longed for his appearing.

2 TIMOTHY 4:8

James J. Braddock struggled to provide for his family by working at the docks in New York City following the stock market crash of 1929, when millions of people lost everything as banks across the country collapsed. Braddock and his family were among those people. This was the second major setback for the boxer-turned-longshoreman in 1929. Having been a successful amateur and professional boxer, Braddock had climbed the ranks after turning pro in 1926 and had become a major contender, but he lost a bout for the title against the heavyweight champion Tommy Loughran only three years after turning pro.

After the loss and the stock market crash, Braddock had no choice but to take whatever job he could in order to support his family. The long days of physical labor kept Braddock in shape, but the meager wages still barely put food on the table. So when an unexpected opportunity to fight Corn Griffin came up, James Braddock took the fight with short notice. Though the fight was supposed to be a warm-up bout and an easy win for Griffin, Braddock seized the opportunity and achieved an upset win against Griffin. Then, Braddock silenced the critics once again by beating John Henry Lewis to gain a second shot at the title.

As a 10:1 underdog, James Braddock shocked the boxing world and won the heavyweight championship on June 13, 1935, beating the famous champion Max Baer. Braddock held the title until Joe Louis defeated him two years later.

Earning the nickname "Cinderella Man" because of his sudden rise from a poor local fighter to become the heavyweight boxing champion of the world, James J. Braddock was inducted into the Ring Boxing Hall of Fame (1964) and the International Boxing Hall of Fame (2001).[1] In 2005, the feature film *Cinderella Man* starring Russell Crowe was released in theaters aptly depicting the hall-of-famer's life.

The old boxing adage "Stay ready so you won't have to get ready" was thoroughly ingrained into Braddock's life. Even after he thought his boxing career was over and struggled to provide for his family, the long hours of hard manual labor as a longshoreman kept the boxer in shape. So much so that when the opportunity arose, he was able to take a fight at a moment's notice.

Well, when it comes to the rapture, those of us who have accepted Jesus as our Savior need to stay ready so we won't have to get ready. As stated in earlier chapters, the rapture of the church is an imminent event. There are no signs or prophecies that must be fulfilled prior to the rapture. It will occur without warning. We are blessed to have witnessed Israel form as a modern nation in preparation for all end-times events, but even that was not a prerequisite for the rapture.

Technically speaking, Israel's national rebirth could have occurred after the rapture. The fact that it has already come to pass should make us excited that the rapture is that much nearer! An added bonus to us witnessing the fulfillment of prophecy with Israel's national reconstitution is that it proves all future prophecy will be fulfilled literally, just as all previous prophecies have been fulfilled literally.

The trifecta of the doctrine of imminency (the rapture can happen at any moment), the super-sign of Israel's national restoration in fulfillment of prophecy (and a necessary development for all end-times events), and the incredibly compelling convergence of end-times conditions in our day should make all believers get ready and stay ready for the rapture.

In the verse at the opening of this chapter, Paul informs his readers that as he saw the end of his life coming, he eagerly anticipated an eternal reward—the crown of life. Though his earthly life was soon to end via martyrdom at the hands of the Roman authorities, the apostle was soon to be more alive than he had ever been.

This reminds me of a famous statement made by D.L. Moody who was quoted as saying,

> Someday you will read in the papers that D.L. Moody, of East Northfield, is dead. Don't you believe a word of it! At that moment I shall be more alive than I am now. I shall have gone up higher, that is all-out of this old clay tenement into a house that is immortal; a body that death cannot touch, that sin cannot taint, a body fashioned like unto his glorious body. I was born of the flesh in 1837. I was born of the Spirit in 1856. That which is born of the flesh may die. That which is born of the Spirit will live forever.[2]

Paul finished his thought with the beautiful reminder to his readers that not only would he receive the crown of righteousness, but so too would all who longed for the Lord's appearing! Paul was looking forward to eternal rewards he would receive via the bema seat of Christ.

One commentator notes:

> "The crown of righteousness" may be either the fullness of righteousness as a reward, or some unspecified reward for righteous conduct on earth (cf. James 1:12; Rev. 2:10). This seems to be a metaphorical crown (i.e., a reward) rather than a literal material crown,

since "righteousness" is non-material. This "crown" (Gr. *stephanos*, a victor's crown) will go to all Christians who, like Paul, demonstrated a longing for the Lord's return by the way they lived. Not all Christians are eager for the Lord to return, since some know that they need to change their way of living.[3]

When I was a teenager, my siblings and I had chores to do each day. After school we would all enter the house a few hours before our parents came home from work, and the expectation was that our chores would be done by the time they arrived home. On many occasions, rather than completing my chores immediately, I would procrastinate until I heard the distinctive sound of my father's car at the top of our street. Once aware of my parents' imminent arrival, I would scramble to get any remaining chores done. I would hastily perform the most noticeable chores, which inevitably lacked quality, in which case I would hope my parents would fail to notice the half-baked attempt.

The idea with the rapture is that there is no warning—no sound of a car at the top of the street. We need to live each moment as if the Lord were to return unexpectedly. If we long for his return we tend to live with excitement, anticipation, and with the healthy realization that we will one day give an account for how we leveraged our time, talents, and treasure for kingdom purposes.

Kingdom Minded

In Acts 1—wedged between a question from the apostles to Jesus about if he was near to restoring the kingdom to Israel and just before the familiar verse where Jesus gave his followers what is known as the great commission (verse 8)—Jesus said to them, "It is not for you to know the times or dates the Father has set by his own authority" (verse 7). Did you catch that? By logic, Jesus implied that the Father has times (plural) and dates (plural) set—including the day Israel's kingdom would be restored (and by extension, other specific end-times dates prior to the kingdom age).

The word used for "times" is *chronos*, from which we get the word *chronological*. It has to do with sovereignly managed sequences. The word used for "dates" is *kairos*, or appointed times. It has to do with specific opportune times when things have come to a head (*kairos* comes from the word *kara* or *head*).

Think of *chronos* as the sequential time a stalk of wheat needs to grow. Think of *kairos* as the moment the wheat stalk sprouts its head and is ready for picking. God is sovereignly involved in both, but God-ordained *chronos* events always ultimately lead to God-ordained *kairos* events—when things have reached their designated end.

CHRONOS VS. KAIROS

If you think about it, that makes total sense. God is (among other attributes) omniscient—all-knowing. He is also outside of time, for he created it. In any case, God the Father knows all the key dates (rapture, return, start of the kingdom age, etc.), but we do not. We walk by faith as we wait.

For the apostles, they were not to worry about it either, because in the very next verse (verse 8) they heard Jesus' last words before he left the earth, that they would be his witnesses to the world—beginning where they were (in Jerusalem) and then ultimately to the ends of the earth. (By the way, Acts 1:8 also serves as the outline for the book of Acts—beginning in Jerusalem and ending in Rome.) This "witnessing" would take time. We call that the church age. But following the church age will be the kingdom age. The *chronos* of the church age will have a logical *kairos* end before the kingdom age can begin. We seem to be nearing the *kairos* moments related to the end of the church age.

As the centuries, years, and months of the church age continue to tick by, we should grow in anticipation of a supernatural event that we are destined for—the instantaneous catching away of all true believers in Christ. It is the next thing on the prophetic-event calendar and it is an imminent event, meaning there are no preconditions that must take place for it to occur. It could happen at any moment.

As we've previously discussed, this Navy SEALs-like rescue operation is known as the rapture. One of our enemy's titles is the prince of the power of the air. Based on the verse at the chapter opening, Jesus himself will invade the enemy's territory and whisk away his bride—the church—from right under Satan's nose.

QUICK FACT: DID YOU KNOW...
that the "S-E-A-L" in Navy SEALs stands for
SEA, AIR, AND LAND?

Generations of believers have longed to be alive when this worldwide supernatural event occurs. We don't know if we are that generation, but one thing is for sure: We have more reason to believe we are close to this event than any other generation in history. First, because with every second that passes, we draw closer chronologically to this guaranteed future event. And second, because all the biblical signs and conditions pointing to the tribulation are forming in our day.

If the rapture occurs prior to the tribulation, and we're seeing the signs pointing to the tribulation period, then the rapture must be drawing close. To use a common analogy, if we see signs of Christmas around us, then we know that Thanksgiving must be near. These end-times signs and conditions have never been so thoroughly in place for any other generation—we discussed this in the previous chapter.

If you have ever been confused about the rapture or if you have wondered about its significance, please read that chapter carefully. As believers in Christ, it is vitally important for us to have a clear understanding of this faith-anchoring event.

Broken Bones and Bridal Readiness?

There is one key detail that I left out from hall-of-fame boxer James Braddock's initial boxing career. As I mentioned, the light heavyweight lost his first title shot by decision. In the grueling 15-round match, Braddock badly fractured his right hand.[4]

On the heels of losing the match, the Great Depression hit. The boxer-turned-longshoreman had to hide his limitation from potential employers. Braddock also had to use his nondominant hand for the bulk of the physical labor on the docks, while his famous but overly favored right hand took time to heal. The result of this setback was that it greatly enhanced the strength and coordination of his minimally used (in boxing) left hand.

So not only did Braddock stay ready for a potential future fight, but his right hand fully healed and he became a well-rounded, two-handed puncher by the time his opportunity for a second shot at a boxing career presented itself. His setbacks eventually served to be setups! In the long run, the trials Braddock faced turned out to make the pugilist a more skilled and effective competitor.

As the church, we are in the betrothal period, and as we wait, we all face trials. It is a time of purification and preparation. Much like Braddock's broken hand and the long layoff during the Great Depression, perhaps the Lord is using these unsettling times to mature the bride and encourage her to get ready. When any believer submits their struggles to the Lord, the trials of life can serve to strengthen our resolve, steel our character, and purify our hearts.

We live in a fallen world that has been in its own spiritual great depression since the fall. At times, we struggle to make ends meet spiritually, emotionally, and for a large number of believers around the world, literally. As we stay ready, heal from our wounds, and strengthen our "inward man" (2 Corinthians 4:16 NKJV), we can rest assured that the Lord is at work in and around us to prepare the bride as we wait.

We can also rest in the fact that God has a broader missional purpose in the waiting. In 2 Peter 3:9, we read, "The Lord is not slow about His promise, as some count slowness, but is patient toward you, not willing for any to perish, but for all to come to repentance" (NASB).

In the mysterious ways of God, we're informed only a few verses later (verse 12) that as we live godly lives and look for the complete fulfillment of the Lord's return, we will hasten its arrival! As we long for his appearing and await our eternal rewards, let's keep running the race with patience and purpose. We must be determined to stay ready, so we won't have to get ready. It is imperative that we strive to live godly lives and to tell the world about the Messiah. And as we do, we hasten the Lord's return and the complete resolution of the story of the Bible.

CHAPTER 15

Get the Next Generation Ready!

The Spirit explicitly says that in later times some will fall away from the faith, paying attention to deceitful spirits and teachings of demons, by means of the hypocrisy of liars seared in their own conscience as with a branding iron.

1 TIMOTHY 4:1-2 (NASB)

Perhaps you have heard of Mickey "Mick" Goudmill, the fictitious boxing coach from the Rocky movie franchise. Or, if you are a boxing fan, you may have heard of some famous real-life boxing coaches such as Freddie Roach, who trained the eight-division world champion, Manny Pacquiao, or Teddy Atlas, who trained 18 world champions during his career as a boxing coach.

All these coaches had one thing in common—previous experience. They all had extensive boxing careers themselves, so they knew what it was like to be in the boxing shoes of those they trained. Furthermore, they were older and more mature and had time to reflect on how they would have done things differently. Their goal as a boxing coach is to pass on this knowledge and experience as best as they can to those they train. They want to equip their fighters with the mental, emotional, and physical training needed to succeed at the highest level.

The Current Battle

It seems as if the intense spiritual warfare in the unseen realm is having a very real effect on daily events around the world. Wars, corruption, extreme immorality, deception, and mass delusional thinking are represented in nearly every daily news headline.

So what should we do? How should we view all of this? How can we move forward without being full of fear about these events and the uncertainty in the future?

First, we must remember that earth is not our home. We are citizens of heaven. We are ambassadors here, using our influence and calling to point people to the good news that Jesus Christ died for their sins.

Second, we must put our complete trust in God. He is sovereign. He knows every detail of everything that is occurring—and he is allowing the prophetic puzzle pieces to fall into place for all end-times events to take place. The stage is being set for earth's final act. We don't know the day or the hour. We don't even know if the tribulation will occur in our generation or not, but we can see the shadows of the tribulation period casting upon us ahead of itself.

Third, we need to trust God's timing for the blessed hope—the rapture of the church. We know it will occur prior to the events of the tribulation period, but we don't know just how crazy things will get prior to that amazing future event. One thing seems apparent: Normal isn't coming back, but Jesus is!

Fourth, we need to remember that we are in the middle of an intense spiritual war that has been going on for ages. And it is ramping up now as we near the end of the church age. Now more than ever, believers must understand the collision points of end-times prophecy and spiritual warfare. We must know how to use the spiritual armor Paul taught about in Ephesians 6:10-17.

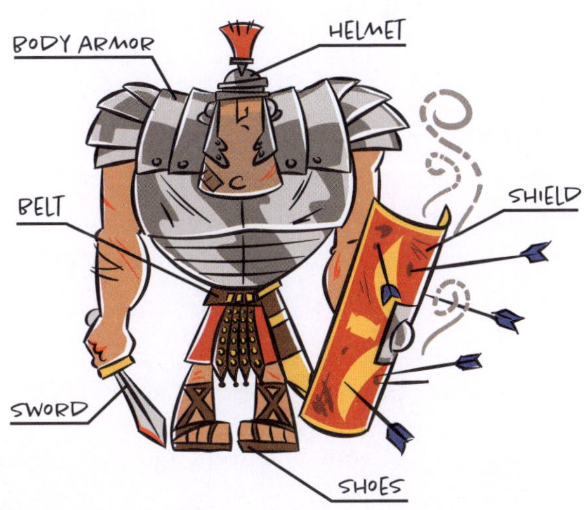

Finally, we must replace fear with faith. Now is the time to put our money where our mouth is. We say we trust God. That is easy to do in times of comfort and ease, but faith really matters when the going gets rough.

As the times get darker, let us draw closer to the Lord. He is our anchor in the storm. He is our rock and our refuge. Let's put our hope and trust in him today as we continue to walk by faith and trust God with the timing and the results.

Let us not lose focus on our main mission—the great commission. Focus your energy on telling others about what Christ did on the cross to pay for our sins. It is a fact of history. We can't force others to accept Christ, but we can lift him up so that others are drawn to him.

Champions Become Trainers—Passing the Baton in Unsettling Times

There is another consideration that occupies the minds of many. Those of us who have come to the realization that this world and its pleasures are passing away understand that life is short and this current world is not our eternal home. We long for the rapture while living with the tension of working and waiting. But there is another pressure we feel. Any committed believers who have children or grandchildren, or influence over youth, are concerned about the condition of the world for their generations if the rapture does not occur in our lifetimes.

Champions become trainers. Those of us who have been walking with the Lord for some time need to take the mandate to disciple others seriously. This call to discipleship begins with our own families. Our children and grandchildren are our primary discipleship target. At the writing of this chapter, one of my adult children is married. My wife and I are not grandparents yet, but it is on the horizon—so I'm beginning to think about what world my grandchildren will grow up in if the rapture does not take place soon.

Protecting Doctrine

Aside from the obvious needs to present the gospel to the next generation and to provide a spiritually and emotionally healthy foundation through the Scriptures and our example, there is another key area of focus that I believe we need to reclaim and pass on—Orthodox doctrine.

That may not seem like something you would typically think of teaching to children, but that is exactly where we must begin. Of course, we must teach it on a level and in a format suitable for their ages and development. But the foundational doctrines of the Bible need to be handed down to the next champions-in-the-making.

They need to know that the entire Bible, from Genesis to Revelation, is God's revealed, inspired (God-breathed), inerrant, authoritative, sufficient, and complete Word. If they are wishy-washy on the foundation, this opens them up to error, false teaching, and deception. Furthermore, we must not only teach them God's Word, but also, why they can believe it.

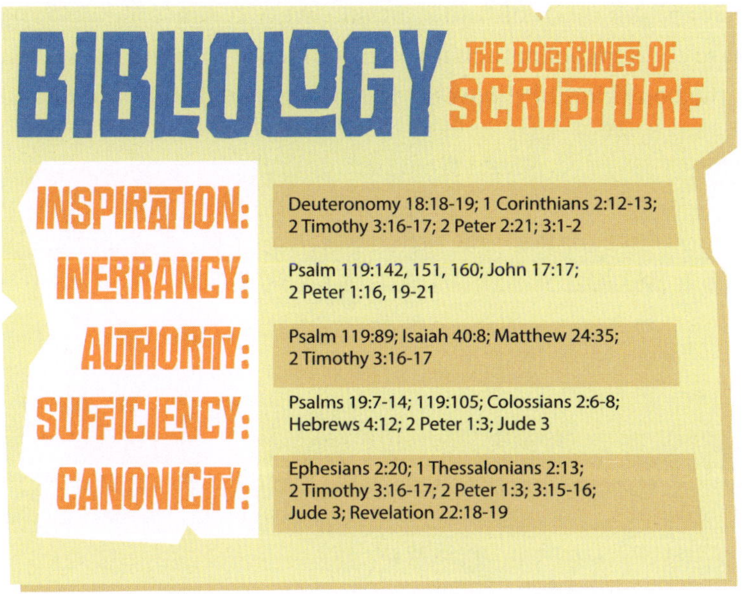

Then, on that firm foundation we can equip them to understand other areas of theology, including the triune nature of God, the person and work of Jesus Christ, the function and purpose of the church, and yes, even Bible prophecy and eschatology! These key areas along with some others will equip the next generation to navigate unstable times and handle whatever the world, the flesh, and the devil throw at them.

In addition to the sobering verse at the opening of this chapter, we find that there are other scriptures that highlight doctrinal error and falling away from truth will become increasingly prevalent in the last days. In 2 Peter 3:3-4, we read, "Know this first of all, that in the last days mockers will come with their mocking, following after their own lusts, and saying, 'Where is the promise of His coming? For ever since the fathers fell asleep, all things continue just as they were from the beginning of creation'" (NASB).

And in 2 Timothy 3:1-5, we are informed,

> Realize this, that in the last days difficult times will come. For people will be lovers of self, lovers of money, boastful, arrogant, slanderers, disobedient to parents, ungrateful, unholy, unloving, irreconcilable, malicious gossips, without self-control, brutal, haters of good, treacherous, reckless, conceited, lovers of pleasure rather than lovers of God, holding to a form of godliness although they have denied its power; avoid such people as these (NASB).

In Jude, the book of the Bible before Revelation, we discover more information about attacks on doctrine in the last days. In verses 3-4, we read,

> Beloved, while I was making every effort to write you about our common salvation, I felt the necessity to write to you appealing that you contend earnestly for the faith that was once for all time handed down to the saints. For certain people have crept in unnoticed, those who were long beforehand marked out for this condemnation, ungodly persons who turn the grace of our God into indecent behavior and deny our only Master and Lord, Jesus Christ (NASB).

Then, in verses 17-19, we are told, "But you, beloved, ought to remember the words that were spoken beforehand by the apostles of our Lord Jesus Christ, that they were saying to you, 'In the last time there will be mockers, following after their own ungodly lusts.' These are the ones who cause divisions, worldly-minded, devoid of the Spirit" (NASB).

If you pay close attention, you realize that these passages indicate that these challenges will come from within the church. The 2 Peter 3 passage references "the fathers" and the 2 Timothy 3 passage says the people with the characteristics listed will hold to "a form of godliness" but will deny its power. The passage from 1 Timothy 4 at the opening of this chapter says these end-times deceivers will bring on teachings of demons. And, we learn from Jude that in the last days, deceivers will creep in unnoticed and we are warned to earnestly contend for the faith.

In other words, as we draw closer to the time of the end, much of the church will have become a shell of what it once was. Those who claim to be Christians will mock the rapture. Many will look like the true church but will in fact be deceivers, self-deceived false Christians. Those of us who are alert and watching are called on to earnestly contend. Those are boxing words. We are to fight for the faith. We are to fight for sound doctrine when deception and error creep in.

In Matthew 7:15-16, Jesus himself said, "Beware of the false prophets, who come to you in sheep's clothing, but inwardly are ravenous wolves. You will know them by their fruits" (NASB). Then, the Messiah added these surprising statements in verses 21-23,

> Not everyone who says to Me, "Lord, Lord," will enter the kingdom of heaven, but the one who does the will of My Father who is in heaven will enter. Many will say to Me on that day, "Lord, Lord, did we not prophesy in Your name, and in Your name cast out demons, and in Your name perform many miracles?" And then I will declare to them, "I never knew you; leave Me, you who practice lawlessness" (NASB).

This phenomenon will increase as the church age winds to a close. But we need not fear the future when we are raising champions. The darker the night, the brighter the light. We need to remember to trust that God is sovereign over their times and their lives, just as he is with ours.

An Unshakable Foundation

This concise revelation from the Messiah ends with hope for true believers. As we continue with Jesus' instruction in Matthew 7, after warning of false teachers and deceptive teaching, the Messiah ends his teaching with this beautiful parabolic promise in verses 24-27 where he said,

> "Therefore, everyone who hears these words of Mine, and acts on them, will be like a wise man who built his house on the rock. And the rain fell and the floods came, and the winds blew and slammed against that house; and yet it did not fall, for it had been founded on the rock. And everyone who hears these words of Mine, and does not act on them, will be like a foolish man who built his house on the sand. And the rain fell and the floods came, and the winds blew and slammed against that house; and it fell—and its collapse was great" (NASB).

Simply put, our mandate for the next generation of champions is to teach them how to build on the correct foundation—one that will never be shaken. We can rest in that simple fact as we sprint to the finish line and await the rapture, all the while preparing the next generation to do the same!

SECTION 5:

THE BEST NEWS EVER

THE CHAMPIONSHIP FIGHT HAS ALREADY BEEN WON!

Get Your Ticket to Ride

Therefore there is now no condemnation at all for those who are in Christ Jesus.

ROMANS 8:1 (NASB)

Imagine someone taking the time to get ready for an evening of sports and competition such as a boxing match. Or perhaps you are more into plays or an amazing orchestra event. It takes time and effort to plan for the outing, to get ready, and to travel to the arena or concert hall. Then there is the issue of parking the car or tossing your keys to a valet. Then, the event-goer must wind their way up the stairs to the doors of the building. All of this simply to get in line to enter the long-awaited event.

Now imagine that person getting to the front of the line of entry and being asked for their ticket. The person checks their pockets, checks their smartphone apps that may have the ticket stored digitally. But to no avail. They never actually purchased a ticket. Rejected at entry and dejected by the loss, the person begins to leave. Just then, the ticket usher stops them in their tracks with some great news. The arena owner has awarded free tickets for anyone who chooses to accept them. The dejected ticketless person is told they only need to go to the will-call window to accept the ticket for entry.

Now, this is admittedly an overly simplified analogy for salvation. Truly, the person must first see their great need for the Savior, submit to Jesus as Lord, believe Jesus is who he says he is (God in flesh), and accept him as the Messiah. But the key point from the imperfect analogy above is that your ticket to heaven is already paid for!

God's Earthly Wrath Versus God's Eternal Wrath

Before someone can understand salvation, they must understand what they are being saved from. As we've been discussing in this book, there is coming a time when God's active wrath will literally fall on the earth for a seven-year period of time, just before the millennial kingdom is ushered in. Yet there is a far greater wrath that we avoid when we bow our knee to Jesus and place our trust in his finished work for salvation—eternal wrath. Better known as hell.

When we perform a careful survey of the Gospels, we find that Jesus himself described hell as a literal place, and our Savior provided a lot of details. Jesus described it as a place of everlasting torment (Luke 16:23), a place of unquenchable fire (Mark 9:43), a place of eternal worms (Mark 9:48), a place of immense regret where people will gnash their teeth in anguish (Matthew 13:42), a place of outer darkness (Matthew 25:30), and a place from which there is no return and no second chance (Luke 16:19-31).

One of the most compelling comparisons Jesus used for the people of his day was that hell is a lot like Gehenna (Matthew 10:28). Gehenna was the city dump for Jerusalem. Not only was rotting trash perpetually burned there, but so were the carcasses of dead animals, and even dead criminals. It was a place of never-ending fire and stench. People stayed as far away from it as they could. That is the point our Lord was driving home with this comparison. He wants people to stay as far away from hell as possible. That was the whole reason for the cross.

In fact, hell was originally created for the devil and the fallen angels (one-third of all the angels [Revelation 12:4]) who rebelled with him (Matthew 25:41). Once the fall of Adam and Eve took place in the garden, spiritual death entered the scene. Hell is the necessary and unavoidable just punishment for sin (Matthew 5:22). It is like a spiritual law of physics. It is simply a reality we do not fully grasp, but a reality nonetheless.

Hell As a Scare Tactic

I've heard people say statements similar to the following, "Hell is just a scare tactic." Is it? Or is it a flashing warning sign? When people see a fenced area with a sign that reads HIGH VOLTAGE! KEEP OUT!, they don't respond to it as a scare tactic. They view it as a warning. It is a sign that is posted with the intention to keep them safe. The same is true for the Bible's teachings about hell. Hell is a reality. Hell is horrible. Hell is necessary. Most importantly, hell is avoidable! That is why Jesus talked about it so frequently. Much of his ministry was dedicated to posting "Danger: Keep Out!" signs. Then, Jesus personally went to the cross to make sure that we could avoid going there.

But as with other teachings in the Bible, the enemy has done a great job of twisting the doctrine and lying about the reality of hell. People wonder why good people go to hell. Good people don't! None of us are good. None of us are righteous. That is the whole point. The real question is: Why would a holy God allow bad people into heaven? Because God so loved the world! God provided a way for sinful mankind to obtain righteousness when there was no way.

How Can I Avoid God's Wrath?

The teaching of Bible prophecy is not meant to scare us but to prepare us. The Bible is God's supernatural revelation of reality. It does not pull punches, but it does equip us to avoid God's direct wrath when it is prophesied. One of the main applications of the book of Revelation for people today is that we should take God up on his offer to escape the coming wrath (Matthew 3:7; 1 Thessalonians 5:9; Revelation 3:10) by putting our faith in the Messiah.

Prior to Christ, we are spiritually dead and under God's wrath. That is not a message you hear preached very often. It is definitely not on the top-ten list of popular Christian T-shirts. But it is true. Once we accept Christ, we come alive spiritually. Scripture refers to this as being born again (John 3:3-6). It is our passport to heaven, so to speak. Do you have yours? If not, please nail that down right now as the Holy Spirit is drawing you. I'll do my best to facilitate.

One does not become a Christian by following a formula, but I've found that what I'm about to share is an effective way to explain what it means to receive Christ and become a true Christian. Some people make the gospel message complex, but it's so uncomplicated a child can understand it. It's as simple as *A-B-C.*

ADMIT

Admit that you are a sinner. None of us are perfect. We all fall short. Romans 3:23: "All have sinned and fall short of the glory of God." Romans 6:23: "The wages [payment] of sin is death, but the gift of God is eternal life in Christ Jesus our Lord." Coupled with this "admitting" is acknowledging that we agree with God about our sinfulness and our need of the Savior. We do a U-turn in our thinking about sin. Scripture calls this repentance.

BELIEVE

Believe that Jesus is God's Son and that he died on the cross with your sins on him. Believe also that he rose from the dead and is alive forever. God was made flesh and died for us to make a way back to himself. Romans 5:8 says, "While we were still sinners, Christ died for us." As mentioned above, this is not merely mental assent but a conscious decision to trust Christ personally. Much like a wedding-day commitment, it is a moment of conscious decision to follow Christ (though imperfectly) and cultivate a lifelong relationship, trusting that he is exactly who he said he is as recorded in Scripture.

CONFESS

Confess Jesus as your Lord. This doesn't mean you will never mess up again. Rather, it means you will serve him and learn his ways as you grow spiritually and as you continue to walk with him in fellowship. Romans 10:9: "If you confess with your mouth the Lord Jesus and believe in your heart that God has raised Him from the dead, you will be saved" (NKJV).

Here's a simple prayer you can pray. These words aren't magic. Again, this is not a formula. But if these words accurately reflect the motives of your heart, according to the truths of the Bible, you will become a Christian. You will have placed your faith in Christ and will have had your sins forgiven. You will look forward to an eternity with Jesus in heaven, and you will avoid the terrible time of tribulation that will soon come to the world. You will avoid eternity apart from God in what the Bible describes as the lake of fire. If you are ready to accept Jesus as your Savior, please pray this prayer now:

> *Lord Jesus, I admit that I am a sinner. I have sinned against you, and sin separates me from you. I thank you that you died on the cross for me. You took my sins upon you and paid my penalty at the cross. I believe you are who you say you are—God in the flesh. I believe you died for my sins, and I believe you rose again. I want to accept your gift of salvation and, at this moment, I ask you to be my Savior. I thank you for this great forgiveness. I now have new life. I now claim you as my Savior and my Lord. In Jesus' name. Amen.*

If you just prayed that prayer, you are a new creation. The Bible tells us that heaven is celebrating right now because of your decision (Luke 15:10). The Holy Spirit now indwells you and will guide you and keep you. You won't be perfect, but you are forgiven, and he will never leave you. His work in you has just begun. You are an adopted co-heir with Christ. You will one day live and reign with him in the millennial kingdom and forever in eternity.

Only a couple of verses following the famous words in John 3:16, the Bible says plainly, "Whoever believes in him is not condemned, but whoever does not believe stands condemned already because they have not believed in the name of God's one and only Son" (verse 18).

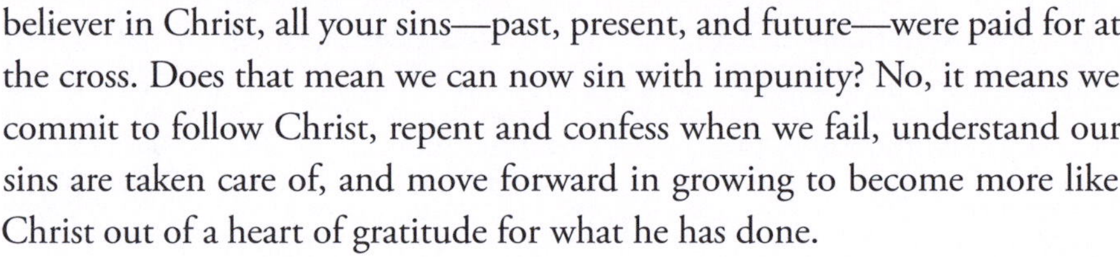

Furthermore, Paul says in Romans 8:1 that "there is now no condemnation for those who are in Christ Jesus." No condemnation. No wrath. No judgment. Your account is free and clear of any penalty. If you are truly a believer in Christ, all your sins—past, present, and future—were paid for at the cross. Does that mean we can now sin with impunity? No, it means we commit to follow Christ, repent and confess when we fail, understand our sins are taken care of, and move forward in growing to become more like Christ out of a heart of gratitude for what he has done.

If you were on death row and someone offered to switch places with you, thankfulness would shape the desires of your heart and drive you to live worthy of the sacrifice that was made on your behalf. What that means for believers in concrete terms is that though we are far from perfect, we are ever aware of the cost of our salvation and want to live up to God's expectations.

When we take time to contemplate how holy God is, how sinful we are, and the incredible price that was paid for us to enter heaven, we can't help but to live a life of extreme gratitude and dedication. This should drive our thoughts, motives, actions, and attitudes. It doesn't mean we won't struggle with our fallen sinful nature—what Scripture calls our flesh—but it does mean that we should be growing to be more like Christ as we move through this life in anticipation of the next.

The Beauty of the Rapture

The beauty of the rapture is that not only will we escape God's eternal wrath in hell, but we will escape his earthly wrath from the 21 judgments of the tribulation period as well. As we have seen in previous chapters, the rapture is an escape clause—but not one made up of wishful thinking or by twisting Scripture to fit our preconceived notions. It is the provision of a loving heavenly Father and the selfless sacrifice of a sinless Son.

Make sure you have your entry ticket! It is a free gift, waiting to be received. Your ticket to enter heaven is also your ticket to ride. The rapture is in your future as a believer in Christ. It will occur after you have died, or for one generation of believers, it will happen while they are still living.

The Savior put it all on the line and suffered the wrath of God to secure the salvation of those who would come to believe. Oh, what a great God we serve. Turn the page to discover what we ought to be doing out of a heart of thankfulness for what the Lord has done for those of us who have called upon his name.

Use Your Feet Before Liftoff

Our citizenship is in heaven, from which we also eagerly wait for a Savior, the Lord Jesus Christ.

PHILIPPIANS 3:20 (NASB)

The closer a boxer gets to the day of the match, the more focused and intentional every thought and decision become for them. One single metric defines everything. One simple question guides every decision: Will it make me ready for the moment when I step between the ropes? This is the solitary driving force for every consideration. A well-trained boxer will exclude all else. Anything that does not contribute to success in the ring is ignored.

The same should be true for believers. As we eagerly await the rapture, we should live as extremely motivated people—with a single driving metric. One question should guide us with each decision, action, thought, and word: Will it make me ready for the moment when I see Jesus face to face?

In the closing chapter of the canon of Scripture, Jesus says in Revelation 22:12-13, "Behold, I am coming quickly, and My reward is with Me, to reward each one as his work deserves. I am the Alpha and the Omega, the first and the last, the beginning and the end" (NASB).

What reward is Jesus talking about? Well, when we compare Scripture with Scripture we learn that there is a judgment for believers—not for salvation, but for our eternal rewards. Since Jesus is coming quickly in the rapture and that is the event we are waiting for, it seems that after the reunion of saints and Savior, we will appear before the judgment seat of Christ to get eternal rewards and our wedding garments.

Paul informs us in 2 Corinthians 5:10 that "we must all appear before the judgment seat of Christ, so that each of us may receive what is due us for the things done while in the body, whether good or bad."

It is a judgment for believers where we will give an account for what we did in light of our salvation. To be clear, salvation is a prepaid gift God offers to those he would redeem. Our salvation was fully accomplished through the sacrifice of his Son to anyone who would believe (1 John 2:2). There is absolutely nothing we can do to earn salvation on our own or lose it once we are saved. But once saved, we remain responsible for our motives, thoughts, and actions—particularly how we use the gifts, abilities, and opportunities that we have been given.

The judgment seat of Christ is not a place where God will show a movie of your life to the rest of the church-age believers—thank God! It's not a tool for shaming or embarrassing us. While our ticket to heaven has already been paid for by Jesus on the cross, there is still great incentive for us to dedicate our lives to his work while we await his return or our own death. The judgment seat of Christ, in Greek, is known as the *bēma* seat. In the ancient world, the bema was a raised platform where judges sat to watch those running in the race to make sure they ran according to the rules. It was also the place from which they would award athletes with special wreaths (i.e., crowns) after a competition.

We learn more about the details of this event in 1 Corinthians 3:11-15, where Paul wrote:

> No one can lay any foundation other than the one already laid, which is Jesus Christ. If anyone builds on this foundation using gold, silver, costly stones, wood, hay or straw, their work will be shown for what it is, because the Day will bring it to light. It will be revealed with fire, and the fire will test the quality of each person's work. If what has been built survives, the builder will receive

a reward. If it is burned up, the builder will suffer loss but yet will be saved—even though only as one escaping through the flames.

Now, here is the best part. Our eternal rewards will have immense meaning because of how we can honor the Lord with them. In Revelation 4 we learn that the 24 elders (representatives of the church) are all wearing crowns. When some of the worshipping angels give glory and honor and thanks to the Lord, the elders cast their crowns before the throne in an act of sheer worship.

The only man-made thing in heaven will be the holes in the hands, feet, and side of the Savior—the Lamb slain from before the foundation of the world. His redemptive work will be a permanent reminder and cause for worship for each believer. Even our eternal rewards will serve to honor the King.

A Compelling Combination

The imminency of the rapture coupled with the lateness of the hour and the promise of eternal rewards should cause believers to adopt a similar mindset. In Hebrews 12:1-3, we read:

> Therefore, since we are surrounded by such a great cloud of witnesses, let us throw off everything that hinders and the sin that so easily entangles. And let us run with perseverance the race marked out for us, fixing our eyes on Jesus, the pioneer and perfecter of faith. For the joy set before him he endured the cross, scorning its shame, and sat down at the right hand of the throne of God. Consider him who endured such opposition from sinners, so that you will not grow weary and lose heart.

In verse 1, we're told to throw off "everything that hinders." This is the Greek word *onkon* (from *ogkos*), which means "bulk" or "weight." The idea here is that we should shed anything that is excess and unneeded weight. A soldier knows you only bring with you what is absolutely needed for the march. Boxers do not enter the ring with ankle weights on. In other words, there are things that are not sinful, but they may not be wise to have in our lives. It's time to shed that unnecessary weight so we can run our race with less drag.

Next, we are told to also "throw off" the sinful things that "so easily entangle." Notice this is not a passive action. Throwing a heavy weight off our backs takes intentionality. We must put guardrails between us and temptation. We must not live in habitual sin. None of us are perfect. We all struggle with various things at various times. But living in willful, habitual sin is like drinking saltwater. It quenches the thirst for a moment, but ultimately dehydrates you even more. Willful sin takes people further than they wanted to go, keeps them longer than they wanted to stay, and costs them more than they wanted to pay. It is a lose-lose proposition.

As we "throw off" we are also told to fix "our eyes on Jesus, the pioneer and perfecter of our faith." As we fix our eyes on the Savior, the things of the world become "strangely dim" as an old hymn says. Like Peter, walking on the water toward Jesus, we will begin to sink when we focus on the waves and the wind. But as long as our gaze is fixed on the Savior, the waves and wind will not have their way.

I want to bring to your attention, as we consider the hope of the rapture and the times in which we live, the reminder in verse 2 that Jesus "endured the cross" and the admonition in verse 3 to "consider him who endured such opposition from sinners, so that you will not grow weary and lose heart." The Messiah set the example. He endured the cross and the evil of the day because he saw what was just on the other side—the completed sacrificial work that secured our salvation! We now persevere because the rapture is imminent.

But What If the Road Gets Tough?

In the opening verse of Hebrews 12, you may have noticed that it begins with the word, *therefore*. There is an old adage that circulates in Bible study groups that says, "Whenever you see the word *therefore*, you need ask what is the therefore there for?" It means that there is some previous information that you need to know. In this case, it is the great faith chapter of Hebrews 11.

These Old Testament giants of the faith are a witness to us on how to walk by faith and finish strong. In Hebrews 11:1-3, we read, "Now faith is the certainty of things hoped for, a proof of things not seen. For by it the people of old gained approval. By faith we understand that the world has been created by the word of God so that what is seen has not been made out of things that are visible" (NASB).

We know intuitively—but accept by faith—that an almighty Creator established the universe. The Eternal One created the finite things. Logic and intuition cause us to know this (see Romans 1:19-20). This basic faith frames the remainder of the chapter that focuses on highlighting some of the Old Testament saints who walked by faith through various trials and circumstances.

The chapter cites key figures such as Abel, Enoch, Noah, Abraham, Sarah, Isaac, Jacob, Joseph, Moses, Joshua, Rahab, Gideon, Samson, David, Samuel, and the prophets.

Then, we read the following in Hebrews 11:32-35:

> And what more shall I say? I do not have time to tell about Gideon, Barak, Samson and Jephthah, about David and Samuel and the prophets, who through faith conquered kingdoms, administered

> justice, and gained what was promised; who shut the mouths of lions, quenched the fury of the flames, and escaped the edge of the sword; whose weakness was turned to strength; and who became powerful in battle and routed foreign armies. Women received back their dead, raised to life again.

Sign me up for that! I want to be part of that overcoming group of supersaints. But not all of those who walked by faith in the Old Testament enjoyed such temporal victory. If you read on, you will discover in verses 35-38:

> There were others who were tortured, refusing to be released so that they might gain an even better resurrection. Some faced jeers and flogging, and even chains and imprisonment. They were put to death by stoning; they were sawed in two; they were killed by the sword. They went about in sheepskins and goatskins, destitute, persecuted and mistreated—the world was not worthy of them. They wandered in deserts and mountains, living in caves and in holes in the ground.

Then, we discover in verse 39 that "these were all commended for their faith, yet none of them received what had been promised."

Can we keep moving forward with one eye to the sky as we anticipate the rapture, but with our feet still firmly planted on the ground and walk by faith regardless of what may come our way? It seems America (and the West) is already under God's Romans 1 abandonment wrath (see Romans 1:18-32). Our culture has plunged headlong into each phase of the Romans 1 cultural degradation.

Will God allow the West to collapse before the rapture? I do not think this will be the case since the global economy does not appear to completely collapse until the third seal judgment (see Revelation 6:5-6). If the US economy were to collapse, I presume that the ripple effect would catch up to the rest of the world in a fairly rapid fashion.

The truth is we do not know how bad things will get before the rapture, but we do know God will walk with us through anything we face. And that it is our mandate to pass the faith on to the next generation. First, I'd like to offer some words of comfort, then I would like to pivot to the question of getting the next generation ready if the Lord does not return in our lifetime—which would be hard to imagine, but only the Lord knows the exact timing of his prophetic plans.

Abraham's Question

In Genesis 18:23, responding to God's revelation that Sodom and Gomorrah were about to be destroyed, Abraham asks God this question, "Will you indeed sweep away the righteous with the wicked?" Then after a lengthy back-and-forth humble bartering conversation between Abraham and God, the Lord answers, "For the sake of ten I will not destroy it" (Genesis 18:32).

Abraham asked the question that many of us are wondering today. If a nation has become utterly evil, will God judge it even though there may be a remnant of people who still follow his ways? After Abraham's question, the patriarch initiated a bargaining dialogue with God. Abraham's request began with 50, then 45, then 40, then 30, then God lowered the number to 20, then 10—and this is where God settled with Abraham. If only 10 people were righteous, God would stay his hand of judgment.

But the only people on God's righteous radar were Lot, his wife, and their two daughters. And as time passed, Lot's wife (who lingered and longed for Sodom on the way out) and daughters (see Genesis 19) would prove not to be righteous, so perhaps Lot was the only righteous person left in the city. Yet in God's mercy, Lot's family went with him out of the city.

The New Testament seems to agree that Lot alone was righteous in his city. Second Peter 2:7 informs us that Lot was "a righteous man" who was "distressed by the depraved conduct of the lawless." He was the only true believer in Sodom, and God rescued Lot before his wrath destroyed the city (see Genesis 19:14).

There must have been a decreed time for the judgment to fall, because there was a sense of urgency to get Lot and his family out. The angels literally, physically grabbed Lot (19:16) and his family and took them outside of the city.

What Can We Learn?

God informs the righteous with advance intel. In Genesis 18:17, the Lord said, "Shall I hide from Abraham what I am about to do?" We also read this in Amos 3:7: "Indeed, the Sovereign LORD never does anything until he reveals his plans to his servants the prophets" (NLT). In our day, the canon of Scripture is closed and we have the complete Word of God. Also, we have God's entire future prophetic plan laid out for us. So today, we who study Scripture learn God's future plans from the recorded words of Scripture.

The pattern of the Bible is that grace and mercy toward the righteous take precedence over the judgment of the wicked, and God extends grace to the latest possible moment before judgment falls (Genesis 19:18-29). We can take confidence that God knows our circumstances, sees the evil in the world, has his own specific time frame, and will rescue the righteous (as imperfect as we are) before his judgment falls on the earth in the future tribulation period.

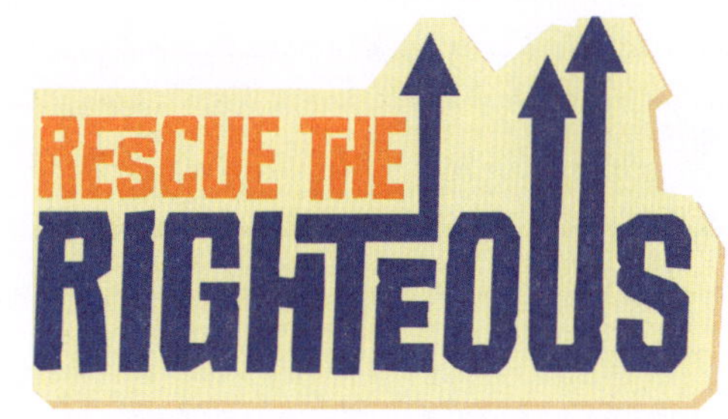

Culturally speaking, we in America and the West have pushed God away. When we push God away, an element of his protection moves away as well, and this has led to the instability and lawlessness we see in our generation. But God sees the righteous, knows our distress (2 Peter 2:7), has given us advance intel, and will rescue us at just the right time.

This does not mean we won't face tougher circumstances before the rapture occurs. We will never face God's wrath, but we may face man's wrath and Satan's wrath to a certain extent. There are fellow believers around the world right now who are facing harsh persecution, mistreatment, and even martyrdom. Yet we are never out of God's sovereign hand or prophetic plan.

When the Road Gets Tough

God is not pacing in his throne room wondering what to do next. He is sovereign over all things. God raises up and casts down leaders. His ways are high above our ways and everything God allows moves history along to its prophesied end. Perhaps God wants American Christians to put our trust solely in him, rather than our comfort and security. God is enough. Really, God is *more* than enough.

Whatever we might face in the coming years, God is allowing it. Perhaps we'll face strong persecution. Perhaps the world will get worse, and our light will shine brighter. Perhaps the Lord will come to take his bride home and we'll finally be raptured out of this corrupt world with its impending globalism, lawlessness, upside-down thinking, and strong delusion. Regardless of what lies ahead, we must trust in Christ alone like never before. He is our only real security and he is all we need.

In Exodus 17, as Joshua led the people to fight the Amalekites, the Israelites were winning as long as Moses held up his staff. Apparently, the battle went on for a long time and as Moses' hands grew tired, Aaron and Hur provided a stone for Moses to sit on as they held up his weary arms. When studying this passage, I've always focused on the help from Aaron and Hur as they held up Moses' arms. But recently I noticed the other key detail—Moses sat on a rock. This may seem inconsequential, but I don't believe it is. Every detail in Scripture is there for a purpose.

Earlier in the same chapter of Exodus, we have an account of Moses striking a rock and water gushing out of it. Later, in Numbers 20, Moses struck another rock twice for water to pour out, but God chastised Moses because he was only supposed to speak to the rock. For this reason, Moses could not enter the promised land. This seems harsh until we realize that God was using the rock as a prophetic foreshadow of the Messiah. This is revealed to us in 1 Corinthians 10:4: "They drank from the spiritual rock that accompanied them, and that rock was Christ." Jesus was only

struck once. He died once for all (Romans 6:10). Psalm 118:22 tells us, "The stone the builders rejected has become the cornerstone."

And in Exodus 17, Moses sat on the rock. His foundation was the Lord himself. Jesus picks up on this theme in his parable of the wise builder in Matthew 7 (mentioned in the previous chapter). If you'll recall, the foolish builder constructed his house on sand while the wise builder assembled his on the rock. The wise builder drove down deep until he hit bedrock, to which he anchored his foundation. Both builders had the same construction materials. Both builders faced the same storm. The only difference was the wise builder had his foundation anchored to the Rock. Jesus is our firm foundation. Unshakable.

Here's the practical application question we need to consider now: What are we anchored to? Are we anchored to Jesus, the unshakable one? Or have we placed our trust in the unstable and temporary things of the world (people, politics, candidates, money, comfort, our country, etc.)? Will we face even tougher times? We might, but if we are anchored to the Rock, we will not be shaken. If Jesus is not shaken, neither should we be. What if the worst happens? What if [insert your worst-case scenario here] actually comes to pass in our lifetime, or even in the next year? Will it occur apart from God allowing it to? No. Will we still be able to live out our calling in this generation? Yes.

In times like these, we need to make sure we truly believe verses like Romans 8:28 and Psalm 139:16. As we head into the unknown of the future, let's take stock in what really matters and evaluate what we are really trusting in. Regardless of what lies in our immediate future, we can't lose sight of God's sovereignty and his character.

We should not be surprised that the world is headed full speed in the direction of last-day developments. Perhaps we're closer to the rapture than most people realize. Perhaps there is yet more time, and we'll have to face tougher circumstances than in recent years. In either scenario (rapture or growing persecution and lawlessness), God is in control. In either case, God will guide us. In either case, we are destined for this moment. In either case, we must anchor deeply into bedrock. In either case, we must share the fantastic news of the cross with a lost world while we still can.

As believers we must not live like practical atheists. If we say we believe God is on the throne; if we say that Jesus is King of kings and Lord of lords; if we say we trust God with our lives and the future; if we say that we believe God is ultimately in control of all things; if we say we believe what the Bible says about where all of this is headed, then we can live with joy, hope, courage, faith, and perseverance—even now. We must not let the deteriorating world conditions get us down. Fear and faith cannot occupy the same space. Trust and anxiety are polar opposites. My first pastor used to say, "Worry is a Christian sin." When we worry, we are not trusting God (see Matthew 6:25-34 and Proverbs 3:5-6).

Let's rise to be the church that God intended for us to be at this moment in history. Though our number is shrinking in the West, we (along with believers everywhere) are still the salt and light of the world. We still have the guidance and enabling power of the Holy Spirit. We are still called to such a time as this. Don't give up now. Seize this moment with our promised future in mind. You'll be glad you did.

The darker the night, the brighter the light. As our spiritual eyes adjust to the darkness, let's shift our gaze from the shiny things of the world to the leading light of Christ, who provides just enough light for us to take the next step of faith. Believer—it is time for your Christian faith to be more real, more grounded, and more authentic than it has ever been. Let's rise to the occasion and sprint to the finish line together. Perhaps the rapture is soon, but if not, we must be tethered to the unshakable Rock of Christ and stand firm in these truly unprecedented times.

Though we may face tough times, the rapture is on the near horizon. Heaven awaits. Let's work hard now while we have the time and ability to do so. I'm reminded of the famous speech that Theodore Roosevelt delivered at the Sorbonne in Paris, on April 23, 1910, where he is quoted as saying:

> It is not the critic who counts: not the man who points out how the strong man stumbles or where the doer of deeds could have done better. The credit belongs to the man who is actually in the arena, whose face is marred by dust and sweat and blood, who strives valiantly, who errs and comes up short again and again, because there is no effort without error or shortcoming, but who knows the great enthusiasms, the great devotions, who spends himself in a worthy cause; who, at the best, knows, in the end, the triumph of high achievement, and who, at the worst, if he fails, at least he fails while daring greatly, so that his place shall never be with those cold and timid souls who knew neither victory nor defeat.[1]

Immediately following the rapture, we will stand before Jesus at the bema seat. Everything we do now has an impact on that moment, and our knowledge of that future moment should impact everything we do now. Let's shed the extra weight, throw off the sin that trips us up, and run with purpose and pace the race marked out for each of us as we sprint to the finish line—listening all the while for a loud command, the voice of the archangel, a trumpet blast, and the distant sounds of graves bursting open!

Maranatha! Even so, come Lord Jesus!

IN CASE OF RAPTURE YOU CAN TAKE MY SIGN.
BUT LEAVE $5 IN CASE I COME BACK.

Introduction—And Still...

1. Ed Hindson, *Future Glory: Living in the Hope of the Rapture, Heaven, and Eternity* (Eugene, OR: Harvest House, 2021), 31.

Chapter 1—Is the Rapture in the Bible?

1. Andrew May, "What is the Planck time?," *Space.com* (January 6, 2022), at https://www.space.com/what-is-the-planck-time.
2. "Ancient Jewish Wedding Customs and Yeshua's Second Coming," Messianic Prophecy Bible Project, accessed May 13, 2025, at https://www.messianicbible.com/feature/ancient-jewish-wedding-customs-and-yeshuas-second-coming/.

Chapter 2—When Will the Rapture Happen?

1. Hank Hanegraaff and Mark Hitchcock, "When Was the Book of Revelation Written?: A Debate Between Dr. Mark Hitchcock of the Pre-Trib Research Center and Mr. Hank Hanegraaff of the Christian Research Center," Debate at the Pre-Trib Study Group Conference on December 10, 2007, posted June 30, 2011, by the Pre-Trib Research Center, Vimeo, https://vimeo.com/25830703.
2. Editors of the United States Census Bureau, "U.S. and World Population Clock," United States Census Bureau, accessed April 28, 2025, https://www.census.gov/popclock/world.
3. Editors of World Population Clock, "World Population," Worldometer, accessed April 28, 2025, https://www.worldometers.info/world-population/.
4. Thomas Constable, "Notes on 1 Thessalonians," 2025 ed., 52, at https://soniclight.com/tcon/notes/pdf/1thessalonians.pdf.

Chapter 3—Church History and the Rapture

1. Mark MacNamara, "The Bittersweet Science" *Nautilus* (December 8, 2023), https://nautil.us/the-bittersweet-science-462168/.
2. Editors of Encyclopedia Britannica, "Boxing," Britannica.com, accessed March 15, 2025, https://www.britannica.com/sports/boxing.
3. Editors of Encyclopedia Britannica, "Marquess of Queensberry Rules," Britannica.com, accessed May 21, 2025, https://www.britannica.com/sports/Marquess-of-Queensberry-rules.
4. Editors of Encyclopedia Britannica, "Marquess of Queensberry Rules."
5. Editors of Encyclopedia Britannica, "Boxing."
6. DAZN Staff, "What are the major boxing titles?" DAZN (February 17, 2025), https://www.dazn.com/en-US/news/boxing/major-boxing-championship-belts-list/ge65lf29o3kw1pmzktuzbad4a.
7. Lee W. Brainard, *Recent Pre-Trib Findings in the Early Church Fathers* (Monee, IL: Soothkeep Press, 2023), 60-63.
8. Jonathan Brentner, "The Most Persistent Lie Leveled Against The Rapture," *Harbinger's Daily* (November 14, 2024), https://harbingersdaily.com/the-most-persistent-lie-leveled-against-the-rapture/.

9. Brainard, *Recent Pre-Trib Findings in the Early Church Fathers*, 75-80.
10. Brainard, *Recent Pre-Trib Findings in the Early Church Fathers*, back cover.
11. John F. Walvoord, *Revelation*, The John Walvoord Prophecy Commentaries, Philip E. Rawley and Mark Hitchcock eds. (Chicago, IL: Moody Publishers, 2011), 300.
12. Michael J. Svigel, *The Fathers on the Future: A 2nd-Century Eschatology for the 21st-Century Church* (Peabody, MA: Hendrickson Publishers, 2024), 8.
13. Norman Geisler, "A Review of Hank Hanegraaff's Book, The Apocalypse Code," NormanGeisler.com, http:normangeisler.com/a-review-of-hanegraaff-apocalypse-code/.
14. Tim LaHaye and Ed Hindson, *The Popular Encyclopedia of Bible Prophecy: Over 140 Topics from the World's Foremost Prophecy Experts* (Eugene, OR: Harvest House Publishers, 2004), 337.

Chapter 4—The Strength of the Pretribulation View

1. Thomas D. Ice, "Myths of the Origin of the Rapture," Pre-Trib Research Center at Scholars Crossing, May 2009, https://digitalcommons.liberty.edu/pretrib_arch.
2. Ed Hindson and Mark Hitchcock, *Can We Still Believe in the Rapture?* (Eugene, OR: Harvest House Publishers, 2017), 83.
3. Hindson and Hitchcock, *Can We Still Believe in the Rapture?*, 83-84.
4. Hindson and Hitchcock, *Can We Still Believe in the Rapture?*, 84. In addition, an English translation of Pseudo-Ephraem's entire sermon can be found on the Pre-Trib Research Center's website: Pseudo-Ephraem, "On the Last Times, the Antichrist, and the End of the World (English)," Pre-Trib Research Center, accessed May 21, 2025, https://www.pre-trib.org/dr-robert-thomas/message/on-the-last-times-the-antichrist-and-the-end-of-the-world-english/read.
5. Editors of Got Questions, "Who Was John Nelson Darby?," GotQuestions.org, https://www.gotquestions.org/John-Nelson-Darby.html.
6. "The Global Need," Voice of the Martyrs (Australia), accessed March 10, 2025, https://vom.com.au.
7. John Walvoord, *The Rapture Question* (Grand Rapids: Zondervan, 1979).
8. Charles H. Dyer, *What Does the Bible Say About the Future?: 30 Questions on Bible Prophecy, Israel, and the End Times* (Chicago, IL: Moody Publishers, 2022), 48.

Chapter 5—Raptures in the Old Testament

1. Editors of Encyclopedia Britannica, "London Prize Ring rules—boxing," Britannica.com, accessed June 4, 2025, https://www.britannica.com/sports/London-Prize-Ring-rules.
2. Editors of Guinness World Records, "Longest Boxing Match" Guinness World Records, https://www.guinnessworldrecords.com/world-records/64545-longest-boxing-match-duration.
3. "3947.laqach, " Bible Hub, accessed May 28, 2025, https://biblehub.com/hebrew/3947.htm.

Chapter 6—Raptures in the First Century

1. Ed Hindson and Mark Hitchcock, "Can We Still Believe in the Rapture?" (Eugene, OR: Harvest House Publishers, 2017), 53.

Chapter 8—The Resurrection to Avoid

1. C.S. Lewis, *The Problem of Pain* (New York: HarperCollins, 1940), 119-120.

Chapter 10—Slo Mo—A Frame-by-Frame Breakdown

1. Sean Crose, "The Fight That Haunted Wyatt Earp," *The Fight City* (December 2, 2024), https://www.thefightcity.com/wyatt-earp-fitzsimmons-vs-sharkey-boxing/.

2. Editors of Science and Media Museum, "A Very Short History of Cinema," Science and Media Museum (June 18, 2020), https://www.scienceandmediamuseum.org.uk/objects-and-stories/very-short-history-of-cinema/.
3. Michael Msilbergleid, "A Look at TV's Instant Replay Through the Years," *Sports Video Group News* (November 18, 2013), https://www.sportsvideo.org/2013/11/18/a-look-at-tvs-instant-replay-through-the-years/.

Chapter 11—The Removal of the Restrainer

1. Editors of New York Times, "Mills Lane Dead," *New York Times* (December 10, 2022), accessed May 28, 2025, https://www.nytimes.com/2022/12/10/sports/mills-lane-dead.html.

Chapter 12—Past, Present, and Future Aspects of Salvation

1. Biography.com Editors and Tyler Piccotti, "Mike Tyson," Biography (November 11, 2024), https://www.biography.com/athletes/mike-tyson.
2. Editors of IBHOF.com, "Floyd Patterson," International Boxing Hall of Fame, accessed May 28, 2025, http://www.ibhof.com/pages/about/inductees/modern/patterson.html.
3. Editors of BoxRec, "Floyd Patterson vs. Archie Moore," BoxRec (September 28, 2023), https://boxrec.com/wiki/index.php/Floyd_Patterson_vs._Archie_Moore.

Chapter 13—Times of the Signs—A Look at the Current Convergence

1. Craig Watson, "What is boxing's greatest and most revered venue?" Planetsport (March 27, 2023), https://www.planetsport.com/boxing/news/madison-square-garden-msg-boxing-greatest-revered-venue-muhammad-ali-vs-joe-frazier.
2. Watson, "What is boxing's greatest and most revered venue?"
3. Watson, "What is boxing's greatest and most revered venue?"
4. "Madison Square Garden—Defining Moments," Hotels4Teams, accessed May 28, 2025, https://www.hotels4teams.com/travel_guide/madison-square-garden-defining-moments/.
5. Olivier J. Melnick, *Antisemitism in the End Times: How the Rise of the World's Oldest Hatred Is Paving the Way for Messiah's Return* (Eugene, OR: Harvest House, 2025).

Chapter 14—Get Ready!

1. "James J. Braddock," James J Braddock.com, accessed June 4, 2025, https://www.jamesjbraddock.com.
2. Mary Ann Jeffreys, "Colorful Sayings From Colorful Moody," Christian History Institute, accessed May 28, 2025, https://christianhistoryinstitute.org/magazine/article/colorful-sayings-from-colorful-moody.
3. Thomas Constable, "Notes on 2 Timothy," 2025 ed., 62, at https://soniclight.com/tcon/notes/pdf/2timothy.pdf.
4. Jeremy Schaap, "Before glory, Braddock was down to his last dime," *ESPN* (June 10, 2005), https://www.espn.com/sports/boxing/news/story?id=2082416.

Chapter 17—Use Your Feet Before Liftoff

1. Kathleen Dalton, *Theodore Roosevelt: A Strenuous Life* (New York: Alfred P. Knopf, 2002), 359.

Other Great Reading by Todd Hampson

The Non-Prophet's Guide™ to the End Times

Do you tend to avoid studying books of the Bible like Revelation and Ezekiel? Does it feel like words such as *rapture* and *apocalypse* fly right over your head? It's common to dismiss these and other topics related to Bible prophecy as irrelevant and...well...too complicated.

But God's Word says, "Blessed is the one who reads aloud the words of this prophecy, and blessed are those who hear it and take to heart what is written in it, because the time is near" (Revelation 1:3).

Prepare to be blessed in a meaningful way! *The Non-Prophet's Guide™ to the End Times* combines engaging illustrations with down-to-earth explanations to help you navigate the ins and outs of Bible prophecy. There's no better time to grasp God's plans for the future—and for you—than this very moment.

The Non-Prophet's Guide™ to the End Times Workbook

Dig deeper into what the Bible says about the end times and gain insight into God's plan for your future. Todd Hampson's companion workbook to his bestselling *The Non-Prophet's Guide™ to the End Times* makes the challenging study of Bible prophecy clear, understandable, and fun.

With more than 100 helpful and humorous graphics and illustrations, you can explore scriptural prophecies and discover answers for your questions about the last days, such as…

- How does fulfilled Bible prophecy affect our view of prophecies not yet fulfilled?
- What can we learn from those who were watching at Jesus' first coming?
- How can we discern between conspiracy theories and trustworthy facts that line up with end-time geopolitical signs?

The Non-Prophet's Guide™ to the Book of Revelation

If the final book of the Bible has ever left you scratching your head or wondering what to make of plagues and horsemen, your friendly Non-Prophet is here to help you read Revelation as never before.

Full of engaging graphics, author and illustrator Todd Hampson has created a user-friendly guide to John's prophecies about the last days. This concise and appealing study

- removes the fear factor and demystifies the capstone book of the Bible
- provides biblical clarity about the key events in the end times
- helps reclaim your hope, confidence, and joy in the promised future

The Non-Prophet's Guide™ to the Book of Revelation offers informative study tools for understanding its prophecies and practical challenges to apply God's truths to your life today.

The Non-Prophet's Guide™ to Spiritual Warfare

Even as a Christian, it can be difficult to discern the facts about the supernatural nature of good and evil. How much has pop culture influenced our ideas about angels and demons? Why do we as Christians face spiritual warfare when the Holy Spirit dwells within us? What limits exist on Satan's powers?

In *The Non-Prophet's Guide™ to Spiritual Warfare*, bestselling author and illustrator Todd Hampson gets to the heart of your questions about spiritual battles, angels, demons, the nature of evil, and more. With Todd's signature combination of lighthearted illustrations and thoughtful applications of Scripture, this guide is both easy to understand and deeply informative.

You will learn to…

- discern between cultural myths and biblical facts about the supernatural
- recognize the real threats you face while remaining grounded in God's truth
- understand why being ready to stand against demonic influence is more important now than ever before

The Non-Prophet's Guide™ to Spiritual Warfare will give you the resources you need to champion spiritual battles, while inspiring you to dive deeper into God's Word to equip yourself with truth.

The Non-Prophet's Guide™ to the Bible

The world's all-time bestseller, the Bible, is truly unique: an ancient collection of 66 separate books written across 1,500 years that fits together like a perfectly crafted puzzle. It proclaims itself to be the Word of God—and supports this claim with hundreds of specific, now-fulfilled prophecies.

Because of its massive cultural impact, readers of all backgrounds and beliefs ask questions about the Bible's context, history, purpose, and reliability. Enter *The Non-Prophet's Guide™ to the Bible*: a bright, infographic-packed panorama designed to give you

- a section-by-section overview of the Bible, illuminating each book's distinct role in telling God's story
- a crash course on who wrote the Scriptures, when they were written, and how they were preserved through the ages
- the compelling case for why you can believe the Bible truly is the Word of God

Whether you're a longtime believer looking to better understand Scripture or an interested newcomer seeking answers about Christianity, this accessible guide provides the insight and information you need to see how the Bible portrays a global history that has unfolded in the direction of God's promises.

The Non-Prophet's Guide™ to Prophecy for Young People

Bible prophecy for kids? Sounds crazy, right? Maybe not. The fulfilled and future prophecies contained in Scripture are more mind-blowing than any superhero story or action-packed adventure…because they are 100 percent true!

Young readers will join the Non-Prophet and his pet frog Plague on comical capers that illuminate the basics of Bible prophecy and apologetics through fun factoids and awesome infographics. Preteens will gain a greater appreciation for God's Word and a deeper understanding of his exciting plans for their lives.

God's awesome promises are waiting for your child to discover!

The Chronological Guide to Bible Prophecy

This fun and informative book provides a comprehensive survey of the many prophecies found in Scripture, underlining their themes and illuminating why they bring us hope today. This resource will deepen your sense of wonder for the Bible's accuracy, while guiding you through a timeline of God's pledges to his people. You will…

- examine completed Bible prophecies—and witness how these unbroken promises create clear and compelling apologetics for your faith
- understand the prophesied events that are still to come and the order in which they will occur
- grow in reverence for our incredible God, who uses prophecy to make his amazing faithfulness known to us

The Non-Prophet's Guide™ to the Book of Daniel

In today's increasingly unstable culture, we need the wealth of wisdom available in the book of Daniel, which teaches us to live boldly and joyfully for the Lord, even in the most difficult circumstances.

Through Daniel, you'll discover what it means to stand for righteousness in a world filled with compromise. And you'll learn how to do so winsomely, in a way that both enables others to gain a clear understanding of who God is and compels them to seek after him.

Explore the many vivid prophecies Daniel had about the days to come—prophecies that shed much light on what will happen during the end times and are deeply practical for our day. You will find your faith strengthened as you see the many ways that God has kept his promises and will continue to do so.

God used Daniel's faithfulness and courage powerfully in his day, and he can do the same through our lives today as we apply the lessons meant to help us fulfill our role in God's divine story right now.

The Non-Prophet's Guide™ to Heaven

How do we know who goes to heaven? Will we have bodies? Will we recognize other people, such as our friends and family? What does having a future in heaven mean for us while still here on earth?

In *The Non-Prophet's Guide™ to Heaven*, author and illustrator Todd Hampson answers these questions and many more with lighthearted illustrations and faithful explorations of what Scripture reveals about heaven. As you embark on this spirited adventure, you will encounter

- historical understandings of heaven and a deep dive into what the Bible really says
- an overview of what happens between now and eternity on a clear, informative timeline
- encouragement to deepen your faith in God's promises and make today count more than ever!

Packed with engaging infographics and bountiful insight, this inspiring resource will transform your understanding of heaven and the afterlife while energizing you to live more boldly in the present.

Books coauthored by Todd Hampson

Answering Tough Questions About the End Times

In a field often clouded by complexity and sensationalism, keeping track of what the Bible says about the end times can be challenging even for seasoned believers. That's why the bestselling authors behind the *Prophecy Pros Podcast* are here to bring you a comprehensive and user-friendly guide to the most need-to-know facts about what is to come.

Neatly organized and packed with charts, timelines, and infographics, *Answering Tough Questions About the End Times* delivers clear answers to 100 of the most pressing questions about the last days. As you learn about what Bible prophecy is and where it's found in Scripture, you will also find speculation-free and biblically-sourced overviews of forthcoming events such as the rapture, Jesus' second coming, and life in heaven.

As you grow in your understanding of God's plans for history still-to-come, your trust in Him will be transformed. Whether you're new to your faith or a longtime student of Bible prophecy, this approachable handbook will provide helpful, straightforward answers to your queries and concerns about the end times, inspiring you to face the future with confidence!

A Visual Guide to the End Times

When flying through dense clouds and rain, pilots don't stare blindly out the window—they focus on their flight instruments, trusting their tools and training to ensure safe passage. In the same way, God's gift of Bible prophecy provides everything we need to navigate the storms of our times with confidence!

Packed with many engaging, full-color graphics and charts, *A Visual Guide to the End Times* provides all the key information you need to understand Bible prophecy with accuracy and certainty. Jeff Kinley and Todd Hampson present complex ideas in a straightforward manner, offering you

- a clear picture and timeline of what will happen during the end times
- helpful definitions and explanations about the many central themes and events relating to Bible prophecy
- a comprehensive survey of the future, presented in a visually stunning and easy-to-use format

As this thorough resource empowers you to trust Bible prophecy and apply its principles with the confidence of pilots trusting their instruments, you will be filled with the assurance and hope that results from taking God at His Word—no matter how bad things look outside the cockpit window!

To learn more about our Harvest Prophecy resources, please visit:

www.HarvestProphecyHQ.com